BE WITH JESUS 365

EXPERIENCE AUTHENTIC INTIMACY WITH GOD

Be with Jesus 365: Experience Authentic Intimacy with God
© 2022 by Mark Jones

Published by Grafo House Publishing, Guadalajara, Mexico
In conjunction with Jaquith Creative, Seattle, Washington

Paperback ISBN 978-1-949791-73-0
Ebook ISBN 978-1-949791-61-7
Spanish-language versions available in all formats under the title *Estar con Jesús 365: Experimar Auténtica Intimidad con Jesús*

Originally published under the titles *Unscripted* © 2013 and *Life-Changing Prayer* © 2012.

To contact the author, access resources related to *Be with Jesus 365* and other tools discussed in this book, or inquire about bulk discounts for churches and Bible study groups, visit www.bewithjesus365.org.

Worldwide rights reserved. No part of this publication may be reproduced, stored in a retrieval system, or transmitted, in any form or by any means, without written consent from the publisher. The views and opinions expressed herein are solely those of the author and not necessarily those of the publishers.

Unless otherwise indicated, all Scripture quotations are taken from the Holy Bible, New Living Translation, copyright © 1996, 2004, 2007 by Tyndale House Foundation. Used by permission of Tyndale House Publishers, Inc., Carol Stream, Illinois 60188. All rights reserved.

Other Scriptures are taken from the following translations. All rights reserved. Used by permission.
 NKJV: New King James Version. Copyright © 1982 by Thomas Nelson, Inc.
 NIV: New International Version, copyright © 1973, 1978, 1984, 2011 by Biblica, Inc. Used by permission of Zondervan.
 TPT: The Passion Translation®. Copyright © 2017, 2018, 2020 by Passion & Fire Ministries, Inc.
 KJV: King James Version. Public domain.

Greek and Hebrew definitions labeled *Strong's* are from *Strong's Exhaustive Concordance of the Bible* by James Strong (1890), public domain.

Printed in the United States of America
25 24 23 22   1 2 3 4

PRAISE FOR THE BOOK

I can think of no one better to offer a book such as this. Having known Dr. Mark Jones for decades, I can assure you that this challenge comes from someone with an amazing heart for God. He is rightly known for passionate, fervent prayer, a heartfelt love for others, and a vibrant intensity in his walk with God. In this book he acts as a personal spiritual trainer with a sincere desire to coach us in how we connect with God. He offers a realistic and "doable" plan as well as practical tips and insightful motivations. In all this, the thing I appreciate most is how he removes the guilt-prone religion and replaces it with a genuine, sincere, and liberating approach. I highly recommend the 40-Day Worship Experience to you!

—*Ken Malmin, Dean, Portland Bible College; Portland, Oregon*

Be with Jesus 365 and the 40-Day Worship Experience will revolutionize your life! I was encouraged, challenged, and inspired by this practical yet dynamic guideline to encountering His Presence on a daily basis. Without a doubt, our lives are enriched and refreshed when we simply take time to be with Him—to open our hearts to the whispers of His intimate love. There is no clearer way to cultivating a Christ lifestyle than through worship. This book is a MUST READ for every believer who hungers for His Presence!

—*Howard Rachinski; Former president and CEO, Christian Copyright Licensing Int. (CCLI); Portland, Oregon*

For the past twenty-five years, my life has been deeply impacted by the life and ministry of Mark Jones. Finally, the secret has been revealed in this riveting new book that has had a profound impact on my own life. I took the 40-Day Worship Experience and am still enjoying the fresh revelation it has brought to my personal devotional life and beyond. This is a must read for every person regardless of age and level of Christian maturity. It will refresh you, strengthen you, and develop a fresh understanding of what it means to have a personal, intimate relationship with Jesus. The challenge is on! I dare you to take it.

—*Marc Estes, Senior Pastor, Mannahouse;*
Portland, Oregon

Dr. Mark Jones is one of the most spiritually passionate and genuine people I've ever met. Dr. Mark's life of prayer and devotion has inspired countless believers, of whom I am one, to transform the discipline of devotion into a pursuit of intimacy with a personal God. His book, *Be with Jesus 365,* is an inspirational and practical guidebook that will lead the sincere reader into a deeper, richer, and life-changing relationship with God. *Be with Jesus 365* captures the heart of true devotional living, and its impact will remain long after the forty-day experience is completed.

—*Michael P. White, President, Gateway Communications, Inc., Portland, Oregon*

Dedicated to my dear friend, Pastor Jack Louman, who passed away on July 27, 2012.

Jack was a true champion of the faith, my mentor, and my friend. He was a man who loved God and family and whose life was dedicated to pastoring and serving people. Everyone who knew him admired him. I'll always deeply miss him.

CONTENTS

Foreword by Frank Damazio	xi
How to Use This Book	xiii
LET'S GET STARTED	1
INTIMACY WITH GOD	
Surrender	29
Celebrate	45
Meditate	65
Open	87
Dedicate	105
Listen	125
Obey	143
PRAYER AND JOURNAL	
Surrender Prayer	163
40-Day Worship Experience Journal	169
Congratulations	251
Appreciation	253
About the Author	255

FOREWORD

In every church there are key principles that become pillars of strength that shape the church. These key principles are usually taught and modeled by key leaders. All truth must be transformed from theory to incarnation. The truth must "become flesh and dwell among us," and there we "behold the glory," full of grace and truth.

Dr. Mark Jones, our church lead prayer pastor, has modeled the truths in this book for over two decades. He has truly let us see the *real* put into the *theory* of prayer.

Forty days of powerful, life-changing devotions will help you take a simple truth and live it out for forty days. Habits are formed in the disciplines of daily activities, and seven weeks may be just what you need to start a new life of powerful encounters with Christ in the privacy of prayer.

Learn to surrender, celebrate, meditate, open your heart and life, listen, and obey what you hear. Learn to journal the work of God in your life.

Here it is: get started!

Frank Damazio
Frank Damazio Ministries, Portland, Oregon

HOW TO USE THIS BOOK

The goal of this book is help you connect with God every morning to receive His love, hear His voice, and be transformed. The book is divided into three sections, which are explained below. It can be used individually, with a friend, as part of a study group, or by a coach or mentor who is leading someone else into a closer walk with God.

The first section, *Let's Get Started*, is an overview of the 40-Day Worship Experience. This should be read first, since it explains what the Experience is and how it can benefit you. As soon as you finish this short section, you should begin Day 1 of the Experience, even if you haven't read the rest of the book.

The second section, *Intimacy with God*, covers seven principles that will help you discover a closer walk with God during your devotional time. This section should be read at your own pace. If you can go through it relatively quickly, toward the beginning of the Experience, it will enrich your time with the Lord. You might even make it part of your devotional time. Alternately, or if you are doing the Experience as part of a group, you might decide to cover one chapter per week for seven weeks. This method also works well.

The third section, *Prayer & Journal*, consists of two optional tools. The "Surrender Prayer" is something I wrote years ago that I always use at the beginning of my time with the Lord to set my heart and mind on Him. The "40-Day Journal" is a series of forty daily readings from Psalms along with blank spaces to journal about what God speaks to you along the way. If you've never done the 40-Day Worship Experience before, I recommend using this tool to guide you the first time, since it makes the process easy to understand and allows you to focus your time on God without worrying about what passage to read.

In all relationships, the connection between two people cannot be easily taught or fully explained. It must be experienced. That is how your relationship with God will be, as well. The sooner you begin to meet with Him in the mornings, the quicker you will begin to enjoy the beauty, intimacy, and love He longs to share with you. For that reason, as I mentioned above, I suggest beginning Day 1 of your Experience as soon as possible.

Visit the website www.bewithjesus365.org for additional information and encouragement along your journey.

LET'S GET STARTED

LET'S GET STARTED

As the deer pants for the water brooks,
so pants my soul for You, O God.
My soul thirsts for God,
for the living God.
(Psalm 42:1-2a)

Years ago, I suffered from constant anxiety and fear attacks. It was a feeling beyond description: a dark labyrinth with no escape. Every morning I would wake up early with panic and depression rushing through my body. I would sit in a chair in my bedroom and worry: about life, about finances, about challenges I was facing, about everything. I thought I was trying to solve my problems, but I only became more entrapped. Later on, I would refer to that chair as my "chair of depression." It was a symbol of hopelessness and despair.

One day, though, everything changed for me. I had gone for a bike ride, something I had started doing a few months prior in order to get some exercise. My habit while riding was to listen to worship music or podcasts on my iPod (which at the time was cutting-edge technology!).

This particular day, I was listening to a podcast. The speaker, in her typical no-nonsense way, said, "If you fall in the love with the Lord again, 90% of your problems will go away."

God spoke to me in that instant. It was so loud and clear it almost knocked me off my bike. "Son, the closest you have ever been to me was when you were in dental school."

That was several decades earlier, but my mind flashed back to it as if it were yesterday. I was a new Christian. I didn't know much about God, prayer, or spiritual gifts, but I genuinely loved the Lord. Every morning for two years, I would go out in the woods behind the dorms and worship for fifteen minutes. I used to wake up the entire dorm with my prayers. It was a wonderful time. I was full of peace and joy. My love and passion were contagious, and people were saved as I shared with them about the Lord.

The flashback ended, and I was on my bike, riding down the path. Then something occurred to me, something I had never even considered before: maybe I wasn't the only one who enjoyed those moments of worship. So I asked God, "Did you get anything out of those times?"

Immediately I felt an overwhelming sense of God's pleasure. I realized that my love for Him and the times we spent together meant even more to Him than to me. I told God that if it meant that much to Him, I would never miss another day.

I had a mental image of God watching His children sleep, just waiting for them to wake up so He could spend time with them and help them with their needs. I realized that the joy, peace, and fruit that characterized my life thirty years earlier had been a product of those times with Him.

> I HAD A MENTAL IMAGE OF GOD WATCHING HIS CHILDREN SLEEP, JUST WAITING FOR THEM TO WAKE UP SO HE COULD SPEND TIME WITH THEM AND HELP THEM WITH THEIR NEEDS.

In the time it took to ride a hundred yards, my life was changed.

The next day, I woke up determined to meet with God. My depression was still so bad that I could hardly get out of bed. I went to a Christian coffee shop, and I started reading a devotional while worship music played softly in the background. Every couple of songs, I broke down and wept. Something inside me found release as I spent time in God's presence.

This went on for six months. Unfortunately, one day there was a fire at the coffee shop and it burned to the ground. I found another coffee shop nearby. I started using headphones to listen to worship music while I drank my coffee and read my Bible.

Each day, I would begin my prayer time with no preconceptions and no agenda. I would simply put on worship music; get out my Bible, a pen, and paper; and relinquish control to the Holy Spirit. My times with God became spontaneous, unscripted, organic, and fascinatingly unpredictable.

Something else began to happen. As I spent time in God's presence, my inner man grew stronger. Depression, anxiety, and fear were no longer able to find a foothold in my thoughts and emotions. Eventually, I threw out the "chair of depression" in my bedroom—I never used it anymore.

I'm truly a different person now. The panic attacks have disappeared. The paralyzing fear and anxiety are buried in the past. I am able to keep my thoughts and emotions under control.

It's been years now since I started my journey. I've kept my promise to meet with God. I know He's waiting for me every morning, and I can't wait to be with Him.

Since then, I have shared my story and the principles I learned with many others, and countless people have decided to try it for themselves. I call this method the *40-Day Worship Experience* because I encourage people to commit to forty days of spending time with God in worship. I have also incorporated it into a prayer class I teach at my church called *Ministry of Prayer*.

I can't begin to count all the stories of fresh love for God and transformed character that friends and students have shared with me. Their changed lives are the reason I decided to write this book. I have included quotes from a number of them in this book.

In the next few pages, I will explain what the 40-Day Worship Experience is, share several principles that I have learned, and invite you to experience God for yourself. My goal is not to control your prayer time, but rather to expand your expectations and release you into your unique walk with God.

I believe the next forty days will change the way you relate to the Lord. If you accept the 40-Day Worship Experience, you will be transformed from the inside out and experience the most important thing in life: authentic relationship with the God who created you.

This book is not an exhaustive list of principles of prayer. I'm not going to give you a formula or ritual to follow. Rather, it's a starting point. An invitation. An encouragement from one seeker to another. The longing in your heart for God is real, and He can meet your deepest need for love.

I like to think of the seven truths we will look at in the following pages as principles that help unlock authentic intimacy with God. Through these easy-to-apply principles, you will immediately begin to practice and enjoy closeness with God. As you do, your life and walk with Him will unfold in new ways. Over the years, I've seen this happen with countless people who have

> YOU ARE ABOUT TO DISCOVER A NEW LEVEL OF INTIMACY WITH GOD.

Let's Get Started | 7

embraced these truths, and I believe it will happen for you as well.

This devotional journey is not limited to forty days, but that's a good place to start! It's interesting how many times the number forty appears in the Bible. I have heard it said that it takes forty days to start a habit, and I hope that forty days of personal surrender will set you on a new course in your spiritual walk.

> FOR THE NEXT FORTY DAYS, SPEND TIME ALONE WITH GOD EVERY MORNING IN AN ATMOSPHERE OF WORSHIP.

You are about to discover a new level of intimacy with God. You will learn how to cultivate a continual inner awareness of God's presence in your life. Never underestimate the power of time spent with God.

What Is the 40-Day Worship Experience?

Here's my challenge: *for the next forty days, I invite you to spend time alone with God every morning in an atmosphere of worship, surrendering your will to His will and receiving His love.*

That's it. That's the whole challenge. The rest of this little book will give you some hints and principles to help maximize the experience, but the premise is that you intentionally encounter God through the intimacy of prayer.

You'll need a Bible, a journal, a pen, and a source of music. I can't tell you what to expect because no two days will be exactly the same. Your devotional time will be fresh and unique each day. This is not a formula—this is an intimate, ongoing relationship with your Creator. Your encounters with God should never become mere duty. On the contrary: they should be the most exciting part of the day.

Every human has innate needs—things like freedom, love, joy, acceptance, purpose, and peace. When you allow God to meet these needs, you no longer have to spend your day in pursuit of emotional, mental, spiritual, and relational fulfillment. You can face your day from a platform of sufficiency. God's presence in your life is the foundation for every blessing you need.

God's love will overshadow you as you delight in Him. Your love for Him will grow. There is no hurry. Let the relationship develop naturally.

To start with, I encourage you to set aside the first fifteen minutes of your day for God. As the days go by, you will probably increase that time because it will become your favorite part of the day.

The closeness you begin to feel to God will continue all day, long after you have left your quiet place. You will find yourself easily slipping into conversation with God. You will be more aware of His presence in every circumstance.

You will actually begin to hear God's voice speaking to your heart by His Spirit, giving you a fresh appreciation for His Word. The Bible will come alive. You will be able to discern His voice from all other voices. The clutter will clear out of your heart and mind. Carnal desires and toxic negative thinking will diminish. You will see God's purpose for your life more clearly.

Devotions Defined

I have always been a person of prayer. I love praying with people and for people, and I've seen God do incredible things in people's lives in response to prayer. I've even been the prayer pastor at our church for many years.

Even as a prayer pastor, though, I used to struggle with finding time to meet with God alone first thing in the morning. I knew mentally that a personal prayer time was important, but the pressures and busyness of life often pushed my devotional life aside. I used to feel guilty because I didn't pray an hour a day or follow strict prayer plans. I even avoided speaking on personal devotions because I felt like I was a bad example.

I realize now that I was missing the heart of the matter. Prayer is more than the words we say to God. Prayer is about meeting with Him and developing a real relationship: talking to Him, listening to Him, worshipping Him, learning from Him, letting ourselves be loved by Him.

My working definition of "devotions" is simple: time alone with God. I'll refer to that often throughout this book. Your devotional time isn't just about prayer or reading the Bible, although it will include those things.

Prayer is someone we are with

The focus is simply being with God. Remember, prayer isn't just something we do. It is someone we are with: God.

> GOD'S PRESENCE IN YOUR LIFE IS THE FOUNDATION FOR EVERY BLESSING YOU NEED.

In the most simplistic terms, devotions are a place to be loved by God. You are already fully known and loved by Him, but in this space, you become deeply aware of that truth. Here is where He meets your most basic need for love. That love fuels your heart, activates your faith, and destroys your fear. It fills your being and reveals the value and functions He gave you when He created you.

All of this happens as you surrender your will to His will and receive a divine impartation every morning. His presence will flow through you, bringing forth His life by the Holy Spirit. This experience happens inside your heart; then it flows outward to impact your physical world with righteousness, peace, and joy. It is God's presence flowing inside you and moving through you. Nothing compares to it!

Set a Time and Place

The most challenging part of the 40-Day Worship Experience is getting up on time each morning and starting your day with the Lord. Often, in the busyness of life, our relationship with God gets squeezed out. We know we should spend more time with Him, but we do not.

(Be prepared.) Everything will try to keep you from these meetings with God. Excuses and distractions will come to mind. Don't let them stop you. Be determined.

> IT'S WONDERFUL TO START THE DAY OUT BY MEETING WITH GOD, AND FOR MANY PEOPLE, IT'S THE TIME OF DAY WITH THE FEWEST DISTRACTIONS.

Establish the amount of time you want to dedicate to being with Him—again, I suggest starting with the first fifteen minutes of your day—and commit to setting aside at least that amount of time for forty straight days.

I strongly recommend setting aside time in the morning. It's wonderful to start the day out by meeting with God, and for many people, it's the time of day with the fewest distractions. Even if you are not a "morning person," or if you are accustomed to praying in the afternoon or evening, I challenge you to experience meeting with the Lord in the mornings for the next forty days. I know you'll love it.

I always ask the students in my prayer class to set aside time in the morning. Some of them don't appreciate that too much at first, but they are always pleasantly surprised by the results. Ericka's story illustrates this. She says:

This forty-day feat was definitely a challenge for me in that doing anything in the morning before I get ready for my day has always been really hard. I don't have too many cognizant thoughts first thing in the morning, and I usually just stumble out of bed, put on the coffee, and think about everything I am going to have to do that day. When I started rolling out of bed and into the arms of Jesus, things could not have changed faster.

Choose a comfortable place where you feel relaxed. It should be free from distractions and interruptions so you can focus all your thoughts on the Lord. This might be in your house, or it might be in a public place. As I mentioned, my habit is to go to a coffee shop, get out my headphones, and listen to worship music. That works great for me.

Consciously open your heart to the flow of His love as you surrender your will to His will. The key to this time with God is to encounter His love for you and to express your love for Him. Psalm 143:8 puts it this way: "Let me hear of your unfailing love each morning, for I am trusting you. Show me where to walk, for I give myself to you." This verse could be your prayer every morning.

Listen to Worship Music

I encourage you to listen to worship music during your devotional time because you are going to connect with

Let's Get Started | 13

God heart to heart, and worship music is a wonderful vehicle for that.

Some people are able to play an instrument and sing on their own, and that is a beautiful way to worship. Listening to a recording, however, makes writing in your journal and reading the Bible easier to manage while experiencing God's presence.

Music of any sort has an element that transcends intellect and logic. Music can encourage relationship, set a specific mood, reduce external distractions, and communicate through lyrics, tempo, and notes. For example, think about the role romantic music plays in relationships, culture, and movies.

> WHETHER YOU ARE MUSICAL OR NOT, YOU ARE A WORSHIPPER.

Worship is more than music, but as we see in the Psalms, it often includes music. Whether you are musical or not, you are a worshipper. God created you to worship. Learn to turn your focus on Him, to put Him first, to value and exalt and adore Him. I will discuss this in more detail later on.

Worship is the greatest act of intimacy on the planet. To worship "in the Spirit" is to know God with your inner self, to connect with Him on a spiritual level. It includes the intellect but goes much deeper than that.

God's Word says each of us is a "temple of the Holy Spirit" (1 Corinthians 6:19). A temple is a place for God to meet with humanity. In other words, He desires to meet with us personally in a one-on-one encounter with the King of Kings. Our first place of worship is not a building—it's our heart.

rhema →

Meditate on the Word

The 40-Day Worship Experience is about meeting with God, and God reveals Himself to us through His Word. As you read and meditate on portions of the Bible, certain passages, verses, and phrases will jump out at you. We often call these *rhemas*, which is a Greek term that refers to a spoken message. These rhemas are one of God's ways of speaking directly to your life.

As you read His Word, you are simply ingesting the words that God speaks to you, interacting with them internally, writing down your thoughts, and putting what you receive into practice the rest of the day. The key is to capture the fresh, living, "today" communication from God by meditating on His timeless and infallible Word. I will discuss this in more detail under the Meditation section later on.

Section 3 of this book, the Journal, contains forty passages from Psalms for you to read and reflect on. I included them as

> **CAPTURE THE FRESH, LIVING, "TODAY" COMMUNICATION FROM GOD BY MEDITATING ON HIS TIMELESS AND INFALLIBLE WORD.**

a starting point, but you may prefer to read something completely different: a book of the Bible, a devotional, or other material that includes God's Word. You might prefer to listen to an audio reading of the Bible, which also works well.

Use a Journal

Capture "God-thoughts," or insights you receive while in prayer, in a journal. There is no right or wrong way to do this. Write as much or as little as you want. Often God gives us a seed thought during our devotional time. If we meditate on it during the day, it grows and blossoms into a life-changing revelation. As God gives you Scriptures, impressions, thoughts, ideas, and things to do and remember, write them down in your journal. Later, take time later to read through what you wrote.

> THE BOTTOM LINE IS THAT YOU ARE THERE TO ENJOY HIS PRESENCE, AND HE IS THERE TO ENJOY YOURS.

As I said, the last section of this book contains a journal section. For each day, there is a Scripture to encourage you as you seek the Lord. The rest of the page is blank and is meant for your notes, in keeping with the open-ended nature of the 40-Day Worship Experience. If you prefer to use your own journal, that's perfectly fine, too.

Be Real

You aren't trying to impress God or prove anything. You are simply making yourself available to God. Don't stress about "doing it right." Don't lock yourself into arbitrary human expectations. Don't let condemnation over "not praying enough" in the past discourage you from starting afresh. The bottom line is that you are there to enjoy His presence, and He is there to enjoy yours.

Recently I struck up a conversation with a painter who was doing some work in my home. He has been in the church for over two decades. He is an amazing husband and father. He and his wife have ten children, some of whom they have adopted. He works full-time at a painting company all day, then does side jobs in the evenings and on Saturdays.

Somehow the conversation turned to a personal relationship with Jesus. I shared the story about my encounter with God on my bike and about my realization that God loves to spend time with me. It was a thought he had never considered before. Even after all his experience as a Christian, the concept of starting his day with a personal, intimate, authentic meeting with God had never occurred to him. He hardly believed it was possible.

As I talked, I noticed this stoic, hard-working man was beginning to tear up. Then I told him that God was available any time he needed Him. I said that every morning, the Creator of the universe was waiting for him to wake up just because He loved to be with him. By now the tears were flowing freely. He couldn't wait to get up the next morning and start the challenge.

Later, I found out that he didn't even wait until morning. That very night, he met with the Lord in a new way, and the following day was incredible as well. As he described his experience to me, he was again in tears. God transformed his world through a few moments in His presence.

The Bible teaches that our lives are safely hidden in Christ (Psalm 27:5). We are seated with Him in heavenly places (Ephesians 2:6). That means we don't have to live subject to the fear and worry that might have plagued us in the past. We have a vantage point to view our circumstances from His perspective. We can see His hand at work, His plan being played out, and His glorious love and power at work on our behalf.

Whether you have been a Christian for two decades like my painter friend or you are just now beginning to know God, you can discover a deeper level of relationship with Him. Every morning, God is waiting to spend time with you. Every day, He has good plans for you.

Learn to REST

For the next forty days, you will set aside at least fifteen minutes each morning to meet with God in an atmosphere of worship. Remember, though, that the point of this challenge is not to get stressed out about a format, a formula, or a schedule. Don't get so focused on "doing it right" that you miss the whole point, which is simply to be with the Lord at the start of your day.

I love this invitation by Jesus to find rest in Him: "Come to me, all of you who are weary and carry heavy burdens, and I will give you rest (Matthew 11:28). The acrostic REST is a reminder to keep our focus on the peaceful, restful nature of this unscripted prayer time by following four principles.

R Reserve a time each morning.
Before daybreak the next morning, Jesus got up and went out to an isolated place to pray. (Mark 1:35)

E Enjoy God's presence with worship music and the Word.
No wonder my heart is glad, and I rejoice. My body rests in safety. For you will not leave my soul among the dead or allow your holy one to rot in the grave. You will show me the way of life, granting me the joy of your presence and the pleasures of living with you forever. (Psalm 16:9-11)

S Surrender your will to His will.
And so, dear brothers and sisters, I plead with you to give your bodies to God because of all he has done for you. Let them be a living and holy sacrifice—the kind he will find acceptable. This is truly the way to worship him. (Romans 12:1)

T Trust the Lord with your life.
Trust in the Lord with all your heart; do not depend on your own understanding. Seek his will in all you do, and he will show you which path to take. (Proverbs 3:5-6)

Change That Lasts

The 40-Day Worship Experience is about getting to know God better. That doesn't mean just meeting with Him every morning for a few weeks and then going back to our old lifestyle, though: it means changing our philosophy, our paradigm, and our value system. It means becoming people who long to know God more.

To achieve this sort of lasting change, we need three ingredients: truth, accountability, and encouragement. Let's take a quick look at these ingredients.

First, *we need truth.* John 8:32 says, "You shall know the truth and the truth will set you free." The Word of God is truth. As you read the Word during the next forty days, ask the Holy Spirit to speak to your life, to change your mind, and to transform your heart. We want the Word to go from information to revelation to application.

Second, *we need accountability.* It's easy to start things but often hard to finish. You see this in health clubs every year in January. The gyms fill up with people who want to get healthy, but by February the numbers have dropped back down. That's why a small group doing the 40-Day Worship Experience together will help you succeed. If you are not in a small group, ask a friend to do it with you. Find someone to be accountable to. Together, you will help each other resist the temptation of the devil and the flesh to drop out of the challenge. Ecclesiastes 4:9 explains it like this: "Two people are better off than one, for they can help each other succeed." A little accountability will give you the strength you need to push through the challenging and maybe discouraging times. We are stronger together!

Third, we need encouragement. Be open to encouragement along the journey, and also be a source of encouragement to others. I have one friend who has his devotional time early in the morning, like I do. He texts me every day saying, "Good morning!" I reply with the same greeting. It's our way of letting each other know we are starting our devotions. It's amazing knowing that a friend is there every morning as I'm rising early to meet the Lord.

Key Thoughts

As I've had the opportunity to share the principles in this book with different individuals and groups, certain thoughts have resonated with people. These are mentioned and explained throughout the book, but I'll summarize them here.

1. The definition of devotions is time alone with God.

This is the simplest explanation imaginable! Just focus on spending time with God every morning. Be intentional and focused, but don't feel pressured to "do it right." Your time with God is not about getting through a prayer list or a Bible plan: it's about connecting with your Creator. That is the purpose of a devotional time.

2. The 40-Day Worship Experience is about unscripted intimacy with your Creator.

"Unscripted" means it's not forced, ritualistic, or bound by habit. Try something new. Do something different. Dare to approach God with no expectations other than meeting with Him. Allow yourself to relax and enjoy His presence, then respond to His leading, and see where it takes you. Every day will be different.

3. God is waiting for you to get up because He's so excited to spend time with you.

I can't tell you how powerful this little thought is for many people—including myself! We need to change our mentality regarding prayer from "have to" to "want to." Imagine a father who is gazing down at a sleeping child. The father is proud and deeply in love with his son or daughter, and he can't wait for the child to stir and awaken so they can enjoy each other's company. That's how God waits for you each day.

4. Roll out of bed and into His presence.

Before busyness and pressures kick in, draw near to God. There is no better way to get prepared for the day than to be with your Creator.

5. Seek God first.

Matthew 6:33 says, "Seek the Kingdom of God above all else, and live righteously, and He will give you everything you need." Learn to build your day by placing Jesus at the center of your affections and putting Him first. We have the privilege and opportunity to daily yield our will to His will and to watch the amazing ways God will lead us.

Next Steps

In the next section of this book, we will cover seven principles to encourage intimacy with God. After each one, I have provided several questions for discussion to help you apply these principles to your day-to-day experience. As I mentioned above, you can either read through the seven small chapters now, before you begin the Experience, or you can read them along the way. Groups who are doing the Experience together may prefer to cover one chapter per week in order to discuss the principles together.

In Section 3 of the book, you will find the *Surrender Prayer* and *40-Day Worship Experience Journal*, two tools that will help you on you journey. I encourage you to read the Surrender Prayer each day along with the selected passage out of the Psalms. Listen to gentle worship music while you surrender your will to God's will and receive His love.

As God speaks to your heart, write down your thoughts

in the journal section so you can remember what He is communicating to you. His passion is to share His heart with you as you spend time in His presence. Let Him communicate His love to you through His Word and by the Holy Spirit.

Now, I want to encourage you to start the 40 Day Worship Experience. Let tomorrow be Day 1, and go forward from there.

Enjoy your time alone with God. Take a deep breath and be still in His Presence. Don't be in a rush. Let these first fifteen minutes with God be a refuge for you. Let your mind slow down and come into rhythm with His heart for you.

You are there to enjoy Him, and He is there to enjoy you!

DISCUSSION QUESTIONS

Take a few moments to pray this prayer, then answer the following questions.

"Jesus, I ask for Your help to go on the 40-Day Worship Experience. My heart's desire is to seek You in this season and to open myself to all You want to reveal to me. I know Your love will energize my faith and destroy fear. I want to delight in You, Father God, and experience the love You have for me. I am excited to embark on this challenge to draw near to You in a fresh way."

1. Discuss some of the benefits you hope to experience through the 40-Day Worship Experience.

2. What time and place you have chosen to meet with the Lord?

3. Is it hard to commit to a specific time each day? Why or why not? What are some hindrances and difficulties you might face during the 40-Day Worship Experience?

INTIMACY
WITH GOD

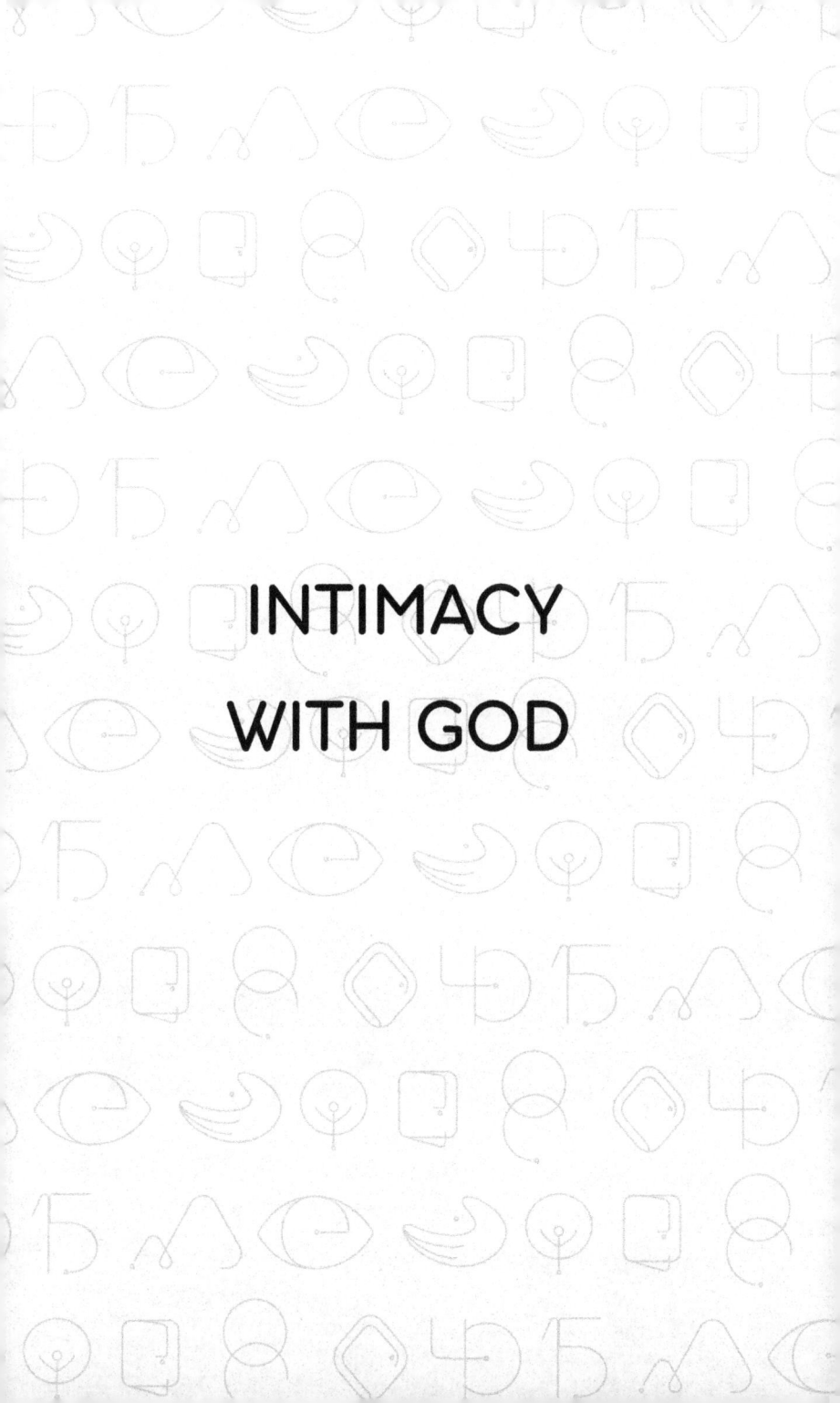

SURRENDER

SURRENDER

**Place yourself in God's hands
and surrender your will to His will.**

O my son, give me your heart. May your eyes take delight in following my ways (Proverbs 23:26).

"I'm having trouble surrendering my life to God, because I'm not sure He can do as good a job at running it as I can."

The young woman speaking was a student in my prayer class, and she had raised her hand to make a comment. She wasn't being a rebel—she was being honest. She had realized that the conflicting emotions and thoughts in her heart were due to her own lack of trust in God.

What stood out to me the most from this comment was that this happened around week ten of the class. We had talked about surrender on week one. It had taken over two months for her to come to terms with the feelings in her heart.

Her struggle wasn't unusual. I'm sure we can all relate—I know I can. It's not easy to surrender to God. Part of the problem is that we don't realize how stubbornly independent we are.

Surrender is our first act of worship, and it is the best way to start our time with God. It is a demonstration of our love, trust, relationship, and faith toward God.

Paul wrote in Romans 12:1, "I beseech you therefore, brethren, by the mercies of God, that you present your bodies a living sacrifice, holy, acceptable unto God, which is your reasonable service" (KJV). The New Living Translation renders the last phrase, "This is truly the way to worship Him." Surrender does not start with an action of the body; rather, it is an internal act, a decision of the will, a heart-level choice to yield our life to our Creator (Luke 9:23–24).

> SURRENDER IS OUR FIRST ACT OF WORSHIP, AND IT IS THE BEST WAY TO START OUR TIME WITH GOD.

Throughout His life, Jesus demonstrated surrender. Nowhere is this more obvious than in the Garden of Gethsemane shortly before His death. In anguish, knowing He was about to be arrested and crucified, He prayed three times: "Not my will, but yours, be done" (Luke 22:42). He knew He had to surrender His own desires in order to win our salvation. It was a defining moment in history.

We have a choice as well. Will we yield to God and trust Him to lead us? Or will we to go through life on our own, pretending we can control our circumstances and destiny?

For the next forty days, I encourage you to surrender to God by applying two principles we find in Matthew 6:33-34: seek God first, and take one day at a time. Live with purpose by starting each day in intimate fellowship with God, giving yourself completely to Him, then let your day flow out of that. Learn how to walk in the Spirit moment by moment, cultivating a continual awareness of God's presence.

The Surrender Habit

To understand the value of surrender, you need to practice it continually. It is not enough to know about it or agree with it intellectually. You must do it. Start every day by consciously surrendering your will, mind, heart, and emotions to God.

It is a simple but heartfelt act, repeated daily until it becomes a habit. Before you do anything else in the morning, find a quiet place to sit before the Lord, as Mary did (Luke 10). Tell the Lord that you realize your life is not your own, that it is unmanageable without His help and guidance, and that you surrender control of it to Him.

A humble and contrite heart is a delight to the Lord. By acknowledging God's lordship, we position ourselves to receive from Him. We clear a path for a successful day of walking in the Spirit. Self-will, on the other hand, is a deterrent to hearing God's voice and accomplishing His will.

One of the greatest tests we face is the daily subjugation of our will to God's will. Once we figure this step out, the rest falls into place. If we don't get it, we will be continually confused and frustrated, lacking inner peace and fulfillment.

Surrender is the only logical option when we realize who we are and who God is. We don't own our lives: we were purchased by Jesus, and we belong to Him. "You do not belong to yourself, for God bought you with a high price" (1 Corinthians 6:19–20).

Truly surrendering ourselves—the good and the bad; the past, present, and future—is not easy. With practice, though, it becomes more natural. That's why it is important to develop a habit of surrender. Check your heart daily. Don't allow distractions to cause you to take control back from God.

Beautiful Surrender

Surrender brings us one of the most precious gifts of all: access to God's presence and grace. Hebrews 4:16 says, "So let us come boldly to the throne of our gracious God. There we will receive his mercy, and we will find grace to help us when we need it most."

How can we, as sinners, enter the presence of a holy

God? And what does that have to do with surrender?

God designed us with a desire and a need to walk in constant fellowship with the Creator of the universe. We can see this in Adam and Eve, who experienced perfect intimacy with God. In every area of our lives, God wants to have access and influence from moment to moment.

The entrance of sin into humanity appeared to derail this goal, but God made a way through Jesus for us all to come to the Father. The blood of Jesus enables us to enter God's presence. That is why Jesus said, "I am the way, the truth, and the life. No one can come to the Father except through me" (John 14:6). He made a way for us. As we read in Ephesians 2:18: "Now all of us can come to the Father through the same Holy Spirit because of what Christ has done for us."

> THE ACT OF SURRENDER DOES NOT END WITH SALVATION. IT MUST BE OUR DAILY HABIT.

Through his sacrificial death, Jesus has become our great High Priest in Heaven. Now we have access to God again. He is our "Abba," our Father (Galatians 4:6).

The greatest choice we can ever make is to surrender our life and our will to God. It is an integral part of salvation. We die to sin and self-will, declare Jesus to be our Lord, and receive new life (Romans 10:9).

The act of surrender does not end with salvation, however—it must be our daily habit. Jesus told those who followed Him, "If any of you wants to be my follower, you must turn from your selfish ways, take up your cross daily, and follow me" (Luke 9:23). That is surrender.

When we surrender to God, we gain much more than we lose. God isn't a power-hungry tyrant trying to control us for His own benefit—He is on our side. He is our loving Father. When we surrender to Him, He takes the broken pieces of our lives and makes them into a masterpiece (Ephesians 2:10). In His hands, even our weaknesses and failures become victories.

Over the next forty days, as you yield your heart again and again to God's will, you will find peace and rest in the plan God has for you. This peace is a combination of peace *with* God, which is salvation, and the peace *of* God, which is a heart at rest (Ephesians 2:17).

Your life will take on new meaning and direction. You will receive a cleansing from all the clutter that has tried to accumulate in your mind and heart over the years. You will understand what it means to "Take delight in the Lord" (Psalm 37:4). The Hebrew word translated "delight" in this verse means "to be soft or pliable" (Strong's). Your heart will become soft and pliable and open to the voice of the Holy Spirit, and God will mingle His thoughts with your thoughts in a new way. Surrendering to Him daily will start the flow of the Spirit in you.

> WHEN WE SURRENDER TO GOD, WE GAIN MUCH MORE THAN WE LOSE.

Resistance

Surrender is the first step to truly connecting with God, but it can be one of the most difficult. As another of my students wrote in a class assignment, "This challenge's hardest part was handing it all to the Lord voluntarily: all the things on my mind, my problems and circumstances, my fears and anxieties."

There are many reasons we might resist surrendering to God. First, *our flesh—our old nature—resists surrender.* That is why we often find our mind suddenly full of reasons why we shouldn't get up early and meet with God. The human, fleshly part of us is supremely self-centered and is in direct opposition to a surrendered life. I have heard it said that the problem with a living sacrifice is that it tends to climb down off the altar! However, the path to real life is to give up our life.

A second reason we might resist surrender is because *we don't realize how much God loves us.* We struggle with the idea of our lovability, so we close ourselves off from the one who truly loves us.

Maybe in the past we experienced imperfect role models of love. Maybe we were abused, treated harshly, or simply not nurtured. Maybe we are bitter toward those who raised us. All of these experiences affect how we perceive God's love toward us. We must allow His love to cleanse our mind and emotions from past hurts. We need to begin to comprehend the awesome nature of His unconditional, eternal, all-encompassing love.

God is love (1 John 4:8). That is the foundation we build upon. When we were still sinners, Christ came and died for us (Romans 5:6). All that we have ever done has been atoned for in the death, burial, and resurrection of Jesus. We are the objects of God's love. God did not create us just to love Him—He created us first of all to be loved by Him. He loves us right where we are.

A third reason we might resist surrender is because *we are afraid we will be let down or hurt*. Our fear causes us to close our heart. Again, this can be rooted in past experiences. We trusted once and were burned by the one we gave our heart to, and now we are suspicious of anything that looks too good to be true.

It's time to let down our guard, to put aside our suspicions, and to trust again. God will not let us down. He will not leave or abandon us, abuse or manipulate us.

A fourth source of resistance is *guilt*. We hesitate to approach God because His holiness highlights our sinfulness. This happened to Adam and Eve in the Garden after they sinned. When they realized they were naked, they were afraid and hid from God (Genesis 3:7–10).

The answer is not to be more holy. It is to receive the grace found in Jesus. As I stated earlier, Jesus already made a way for us to approach the Father—not on our merit, but through Him. Approach God with boldness, and surrender to Him without fear that He will punish you for past errors. He is waiting with open, forgiving arms.

Whatever the source of your resistance might be, and whether it is conscious or subconscious, it is time to let it go. Maybe you have felt like you are caught in a rut in your walk with God. I believe you are reading this for a purpose. Your heart has been stirred to go deeper with God because He is about to do something new in you. You must believe that old things have passed away and new things are coming (2 Corinthians 5:17). God has so much more for you, and you have been sensing that in your heart.

> DON'T SETTLE FOR THE SAME RELATIONSHIP WITH GOD THAT YOU'VE HAD FOR YEARS.

This is not a time to pull back in your pursuit of God—this is a time to press in. Read Jeremiah 29:11-12. God promises you a wonderful future, but you must surrender to His plans and His future for you.

Don't settle for the same relationship with God that you've had for years. It is time to accept the challenge and do something different—not out of duty or obligation, but out of passion to find God in a new way and to draw near to Him.

There is always more in God. His love and goodness are endless! As Paul says in Ephesians 3:18, "May you have the power to understand, as all God's people should, how wide, how long, how high, and how deep his love is."

Do as King David did in Psalm 42:1—thirst for God like a deer searching for the water brook. Let your thirst be for Him and Him alone. Don't let anything get between you and His love.

I challenge you to try it. Every morning during these forty days, surrender your will to His will, and see what God does. I did, and it changed my life forever! What do you have to lose? Maybe a little sleep, but that is a small thing compared to all that Jesus is about to do in your life.

One last thing. I wrote a surrender prayer during my journey of meeting with the Lord in the mornings, and I've included it here (see pages 163-167). Over the years, I've added to it as I was prompted by the Holy Spirit. There are many Scripture references you can look up if you'd like to see the passage the prayer was based on. I love to pray this daily as I begin my time with the Lord. I've included it as a starting point for your prayer time, if you'd like to use it. You might even want to add to it or let it inspire you to write your own. It's completely up to you!

SURRENDER

Chapter Summary

Surrendering to God may be the biggest challenge of all, but it is the key that opens us up to God's destiny for us.

Surrendering our will to God's perfect will requires a personal choice. We relinquish control of all we are and ever will be to the one who purchased us, our Lord Jesus Christ. He becomes the center of our life. He becomes Lord. We place Him on the throne of our heart, thus dethroning the greatest enemy we face: our own self-will.

Surrender is a key to walking with God. It's not just something we do at salvation. It's a moment-by-moment decision, a lifestyle, a habit. You might find it challenging at first, but over time you will see the power of God that is released as you yield your life.

I am reminded of the rich young ruler (Mark 10:17-22). He was told by Jesus to sell all he had and follow Jesus. The ruler was sad because he had so much and the sacrifice seemed too great. That day, his will got in the way of his destiny.

The disciples faced the same choice when Jesus said to them, "Follow me." They left everything and followed Him, and it was the first step toward a lifetime of relationship with Jesus.

Picture a door with your destiny behind it. You hold the key to open that door: it is surrender.

Discussion Questions

Take a few moments to pray this prayer, then answer the following questions.

"Jesus, I surrender my will to Your will in this moment. Forgive me for the times I have been self-willed and stubbornly tried to do things my way. I see the importance of yielding to Your will and receiving Your grace to guide my life. My life is not my own anymore, and You are the Lord of my life. Please lead me by the Holy Spirit and help me be sensitive to Your heart today."

1. Are you having a hard time surrendering your will to God? Why or why not? Do you view surrender as a positive or negative concept?

2. Read Roman 12:1 aloud. What does this verse mean to you?

   And so, dear brothers and sisters, I plead with you to give your bodies to God because of all he has done for you. Let them be a living and holy sacrifice—the kind he will find acceptable. This is truly the way to worship him. (Romans 12:1 NLT)

3. Read 1 Corinthians 6:19-20. What does the phrase "you do not belong to yourself" mean to you?

   Don't you realize that your body is the temple of the Holy Spirit, who lives in you and was given to you by God? You do not belong to yourself, for God bought you with a high price. So you must honor God with your body. (1 Corinthians 6:19-20)

4. Read Luke 9:23–24. How do the words of Jesus relate to surrender?

   Then he said to the crowd, "If any of you wants to be my follower, you must give up your own way, take up your cross daily, and follow me. If you try to hang on to your life, you will lose it. But if you give up your life for my sake, you will save it. (Luke 9:23-24)

Your Mornings So Far

1. What are some challenges you've faced during the 40-Day Worship Experience?

2. What is happening in your heart, and what is God speaking to you?

3. What changes do you see happening in your life?

CELEBRATE

CELEBRATE

Listen to worship music and enjoy who God is and what He has done.

Rise up, O LORD, in all your power. With music and singing we celebrate your mighty acts (Psalm 21:13).

Worship is a heart issue that begins with a surrendered will, as I discussed in the previous pages. But in its most expressive form, worship is a vocal, musical celebration of who God is and what He has done (Psalm 150). Ephesians 5:18–19 says, "Don't be drunk with wine, because it will ruin your life. Instead, be filled with the Holy Spirit, singing psalms and hymns and spiritual songs among yourselves, and making music to the Lord in your heart."

Built to Worship

God has created us to worship Him with joy and admiration. We can choose to express our feelings for Him with heartfelt words and music. Even people who consider themselves non-musical enjoy different forms of music. Somehow, the beauty and poetry of notes, rhythm, and lyrics allow us to express feelings that are hard to put into words.

Celebrating His love and goodness every morning will revolutionize our relationship with Him. If we desire to develop a continual awareness of His presence, worship and music are crucial.

One young woman who recently took the 40-Day Worship Experience told me, "I definitely connect best with simple worship unto Him. I love worship because it brings an overwhelming sense of surrender. It declares that He is God and I am not."

All of us worship something. It might be God, our spouse, happiness, a career, or just about anything that takes first place in our life. The object of our worship deeply affects the course of our life for two reasons. First, since worship directs the focus of our heart and thoughts, whom or what we worship controls us. Second, we tend to become like the thing or person we worship. We naturally pattern our lifestyle, values, and choices after whomever or whatever we idolize.

> WHEN WE UNDERSTAND THE AMAZING GRACE GOD OFFERS US THROUGH JESUS, OUR NATURAL RESPONSE IS JOY, GRATITUDE, AND HEARTFELT CELEBRATION.

When we set God first by daily surrendering our will (Matthew 6:33), we make God the focus of our worship. He becomes the prime influencer in our lives. His identity becomes imprinted on ours, and His desires guide and shape us. As the Bible says, we are changed into His image. "And the Lord—who is the Spirit—makes us more and more like him as we are changed into his glorious image" (2 Corinthians 3:18).

Intimacy begins with a face-to-face encounter. When we encounter Him through worship, we are transformed as His light and love shine in us (Ephesians 1:18). Transformation is a byproduct of spending time in His presence.

A Reason to Celebrate

In these moments with God, we celebrate who He is. We rejoice in all He has done, all He is doing, and all He will do for us. Celebrating the good things we have received with thanksgiving is the best way I have found to defeat negative thoughts and emotions.

The greatest gift God has given us is salvation (Ephesians 2:4–10). When we understand the amazing grace God offers us through Jesus, our response is joy, gratitude, and heartfelt celebration.

God created us to be in His presence, to enjoy fellowship and intimacy with Him. When sin entered the human race, it brought instant separation from God. God is holy, and sin cannot remain in His presence.

Yet, God loved the world so much that He couldn't leave things that way. He provided a way for us to return to Him through Jesus. Jesus lived a perfect life, so He did not deserve death. However, He died in our place, then He conquered death by rising from the dead.

At the time of Jesus' life and death, there was a thick veil or curtain in the temple in Jerusalem that separated the Most Holy Place (where God's presence resided) from the rest of the temple. This veil represented the separation between God and man. Because of sin, man did not have free access to God.

> WE HAVE MANY REASONS TO CELEBRATE, BUT THE GREATEST OF ALL IS GOD'S GIFT OF FORGIVENESS AND RESTORED RELATIONSHIP.

When Jesus took His last breath on the cross, the earth shook violently, and the veil in the Temple was split in two (Matthew 27:51). It was ripped supernaturally from top to bottom, signifying that God was opening a way for humanity to have a relationship with Him.

Just like the temple veil, the spiritual separation between God and humanity was torn down through the blood of Jesus. He made atonement, or payment, once and for all for all our sins. Ephesians 2:18 says, "Now all of us can come to the Father through the same Holy Spirit because of what Christ has done for us." Jesus' death and resurrection made a way for us to return to an intimate, ongoing relationship with our Creator.

We have many reasons to celebrate, but the greatest of all is God's gift of forgiveness and restored relationship. During the 40-Day Worship Experience, I encourage you to reflect on this gift of grace and to celebrate your freedom to enjoy His presence (2 Corinthians 3:17).

You the Worshipper

I don't have a musical bone in my body. Years ago, I took a few guitar lessons. After several painful weeks, the guitar teacher said, "God has given you gifts, but I don't think playing a musical instrument is one of them." That was true, but it was hard to hear!

I love music, especially worshipping the Lord with music. You don't have to be musical to be a worshipper, though. Through today's technology, everyone has access to the greatest collection of worship music ever amassed.

Some people can create beautiful music on their own, and others can use beautiful music that has been produced by others to assist them in making music to the Lord in their heart. Either way, music is a key to our worship and our celebration of everything Jesus has done and will do.

I am rather technologically challenged, so when I first began this journey, I had a friend set up an iPod for me. I loved it—each morning, within seconds, worship music filled my ears, and I found myself once again in God's presence. The electronic device I use has changed over the years, but one thing remains the same: the beautiful, intimate sense of God's presence as I allow music to set the atmosphere.

The point of the 40-Day Worship Experience is to spend time with God, not to impress Him with our musical ability. Worship music is simply a doorway into His presence. Utilize it however is best for you. In fact, even if you know how to play an instrument, you might find it less distracting to set it aside during these morning devotional times and put on worship music. That will free your hands up to write in your journal.

In order to worship daily, you need to have a plan. Many of us wake up a little cloudy in the morning—maybe even depressed, anxious, or discouraged. The cares of the day are waiting for us the moment our eyes open, and our natural tendency is to either hide from them or try to solve them in our own strength. Prayer—especially celebrating Jesus through worship—is often the last thing on our mind.

That's where preparation comes in. Have a set place where you go to seek the Lord each morning. Keep your Bible, worship music, journal, and pen together and ready to go. The idea is to roll out of bed and into His presence. Whether you feel "worshipful" or not, put on your music. Allow the music to minister to you as you surrender your will to His. Turn your mind toward God, giving Him your cares and worries (1 Peter 5:7). Let your heart begin to sing the songs that are being played and open yourself up to God's heart. Celebrate Jesus with the words of the songs.

Depending on where you are, you might want to sing along. You can also make up your own words—in essence, singing your praise. Or, you might remain silent and allow the words to minister to you. Often, a certain phrase will stand out, and you will focus on that for some time, meditating on the truth in it, while the music continues. Other times the Holy Spirit will speak something to your heart that is completely unrelated to the music. Be ready to write down what He says in the Journal.

> REGARDLESS OF THE FORM YOUR WORSHIP TIME TAKES, YOU WILL FIND THAT THE ATMOSPHERE OF WORSHIP MUSIC PREPARES YOUR HEART TO RECEIVE FROM GOD.

Regardless of the form your worship time takes, you will find that the atmosphere of worship music prepares your heart to receive from God. The Psalmist writes, "Enter his gates with thanksgiving; go into his courts with praise. Give thanks to him and praise his name" (Psalm 100:4).

The dynamic of worship through music is one of the best ways to experience the presence of the Holy Spirit. Ephesians 5:18 speaks of being filled with the Spirit. The idea here is a continual presence of the Spirit like a flowing fountain. It is an ongoing release of God's Spirit in us.

This is often called the flow of the Spirit, and until you have experienced it, it's hard to describe. It is a gentle interaction between the Holy Spirit and our heart. It is an awareness that God is right there, actively speaking to us and spending time with us. It is an experience with Him.

The flow is His presence in our life, which happens with our permission. Jesus said, "Rivers of living water will flow from [your] heart" (John 7:38). We experience the life of God flowing through us as we come to Him with a heart of surrender.

> BEING FILLED WITH THE SPIRIT IS MORE THAN AN EMOTIONAL EXPERIENCE. IT IS A CATALYST FOR TRANSFORMATION.

When we begin to flow in the Spirit, prayer becomes completely natural. We don't have to force or fabricate anything. We find ourselves in His presence, delighting in Him, alternately talking and listening, singing and sitting in silence.

Being filled with the Spirit is more than an emotional experience. It is a catalyst for transformation. Ephesians 5:19, which we read earlier, refers to "making music to the Lord in your hearts." The heart is the center of our thoughts, feelings, choices, attitudes, and beliefs. It is the fertile place inside us where God's word takes root and grows (Luke 8:11–15).

Romans 12:2 says, "Let God transform you into a new person by changing the way you think." Meditating in worship on the multifaceted goodness of God restores our thoughts and emotions. It's like rebooting our mind.

The flow or filling of the Holy Spirit in our devotional time will spill over into every area. Throughout the day, we will find it easier to hear the Spirit's voice, to make wise choices, to resist temptation, to see as Jesus would see, to walk in the fruit of the Spirit (Galatians 5:22-23), and to function in the gifts of the Spirit (Romans 12:6-8).

FOCUS

Colossians 3:1 says, "Set your affection on things above, not on things on the earth" (KJV). This speaks of focus: fixing our attention, values, and passion on the Lord. It is the fulfillment of Matthew 6:33 (seeking first the Kingdom of God) at the very start of the day.

The goal is to get our day started with God at the center of our heart's affections. The word FOCUS is a simple acrostic that describes the process of growing in intimacy.

F   Fix your gaze.
We do this by keeping our eyes on Jesus, the champion who initiates and perfects our faith. (Hebrews 12:2)

O   Open your heart.
Look! I stand at the door and knock. If you hear my voice and open the door, <u>I will come in</u>, and we will share a meal together as friends. (Revelation 3:20)

C   Connect to His Spirit.
But it was to us that God revealed these things by his Spirit. For his Spirit searches out everything and shows us God's deep secrets. (1 Corinthians 2:10)

U   Usher in His presence.
So let us come boldly to the throne of our gracious God. There we will receive his mercy, and we will find grace to help us when we need it most. (Hebrews 4:16)

S   Start the flow.
Anyone who believes in me may come and drink! For the Scriptures declare, "Rivers of living water will flow from his heart." (John 7:38)

Fix Your Gaze

Start by focusing on Jesus while listening to worship music. Hebrews 12:2 speaks of "fixing our eyes on Jesus, the pioneer and perfecter of faith" (NIV). The Greek word for "fix" means "to consider attentively;" it comes from the word "to stare at" (Strong's). Intently focus your eyes on Jesus. Don't be discouraged if your mind wanders sometimes—just refocus. He is always looking at you, of course. Now you are simply looking back, face to face (Exodus 33:11). It's the best possible way to start the day.

Open Your Heart

Worship is a blend of surrender and passion. As the music continues playing, open your heart to the Lord. Revelation 3:20 says, "Look! I stand at the door and knock. If you hear my voice and open the door, I will come in, and we will share a meal together as friends." Picture yourself going to the door and opening it up to the Lord and His love for you. Mary sat at Jesus' feet and listened, as should we (Luke 10:39). God wants to make His home in our heart (Ephesians 3:17).

Connect to His Spirit

God wants to connect His Spirit to your heart. This is accomplished in intimate moments of surrender and divine exchange. These moments cannot be described in human terms because they are the interaction of God's Spirit and our heart.

Don't back off because of doubts, fears, or insecurities. If you start to feel any new emotions, don't overreact. Keep focusing on Jesus, His love for you, and your love for Him.

Usher in His Presence

God is always present. But there is a deeper level of His presence that occurs when our innermost being encounters the Spirit of the living God. This is more than an emotion, although it will almost certainly involve our emotions. It is the real, tangible, powerful presence of God.

In society, the average person has little or no access to high-ranking government authorities. Any access is tightly controlled and must observe strict protocol. Not so with our heavenly ruler, God. Hebrews 4:16 tells us that we can come boldly before Him whenever we want, and we can ask for whatever we need.

Consciously and intentionally remind yourself of His presence. Open up your heart and allow yourself to experience His presence. Believe that He loves you, that He delights to be with you, and that He wants you to be happy and fulfilled. God isn't just the creator of the earth: He is your creator, and He is overjoyed to spend time with you.

Start the Flow

From here, it's a flow. You might flow into prayer (either petition or intercession), or you might just keep listening. As the music continues playing, stay open to the flow of the Holy Spirit and what God is directing. You will know when this flow of God's Spirit begins. It is the very life of God moving through you, bringing about a divine exchange: His strength for your weakness (Isaiah 40:31).

If there is anything hindering the flow of His Spirit, the Lord will speak to your heart. He wants fellowship with you, and sin hinders that relationship. If you are listening to His voice, He will convict you of wrongdoing or hidden sin and reveal any other hindrance to the relationship.

If this occurs, simply respond to what you are sensing. Ask His forgiveness and receive His love. Let the grace you need flow into your heart. You will have clean hands and a pure heart to receive His presence (Psalm 24:3-6).

Respond practically to the leading of the Holy Spirit. If a particular song ministers to you, repeat it a time or two. If you are led to read your Bible or a certain devotional book or perhaps to write in your journal, then do so.

God wants us to experience the incredible depths of His love. As David says, "taste and see that the Lord is good" (Psalm 34:8). In God we find fulfillment for our human needs of freedom, love, acceptance, peace, joy, and purpose. The Bible sums it up this way: "In him we live and move and exist" (Acts 17:28).

If you have been a recipient of God's goodness—which we all have—take time to express your gratitude and worship. God will respond to your celebration of Him. As James 4:8 says, "Come close to God, and God will come close to you."

Begin each of the next forty days in unscripted intimacy by yielding your will to His perfect will, listening to worship music, and celebrating what Jesus has done for you.

His goodness is worth celebrating!

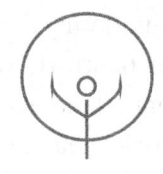

CELEBRATE

Chapter Summary

The most exciting part about the 40-Day Worship Experience is spending intimate time in the morning with the Lord. As we fix our focus on Him and open our heart to His love, the Holy Spirit begins to interact with our mind, will, and emotions. The atmosphere of worship ushers in His presence and allows the Spirit of God to start a fresh flow of communion with us.

God has initiated the relationship with us by sending His Son to die in our place. We now have companionship with a loving God. Focus your worship on enjoying God's presence as He enjoys yours. Think more about Him than about yourself. Thank Him for His grace and righteousness rather than wasting time and energy on condemnation. Remember, you have been set free from condemnation through Jesus (Romans 8:1), and now you can talk directly and continually with your Creator just as God always wanted.

As you go to bed each night, remember God is waiting for you to wake up. He can't wait to spend time with you. I find the anticipation for the morning starts the night before because I know that this time is reserved just for God.

Discussion Questions

Take a few moments to pray this prayer, then answer the following questions.

"This is a day that You have made, and I will rejoice and be glad in it! Today I am excited to celebrate who You are and all You have done for me. I am grateful for my salvation through Jesus, and I want to express my heart to You in praise and thanksgiving. I enjoy being with You, experiencing Your goodness and kindness. You are the focus of my affection, and my thoughts are fixed on You. My heart is full today. I lift up a song to You in celebration of Your majesty."

1. What effect does worship music have on your heart as you spend time with God?

2. Read Hebrews 4:16 aloud. What does this verse mean to you?

   So let us come boldly to the throne of our gracious God. There we will receive his mercy, and we will find grace to help us when we need it most. (Hebrew 4:16)

3. Is it hard for you to receive God's love? What hinders you from coming boldly before the Lord? Do you still feel guilty? Why or why not?

4. Read Ephesians 2:18 and 2 Corinthians 3:16-18. What do these verses tell you about the access you have to God's presence?

   Now all of us can come to the Father through the same Holy Spirit because of what Christ has done for us. (Ephesians 2:18)

But whenever someone turns to the Lord, the veil is taken away. For the Lord is the Spirit, and wherever the Spirit of the Lord is, there is freedom. So all of us who have had that veil removed can see and reflect the glory of the Lord. And the Lord—who is the Spirit—makes us more and more like him as we are changed into his glorious image. (2 Corinthians 3:16-18)

Your Mornings So Far

1. What are some challenges you've faced during the 40-Day Worship Experience?

2. What is happening in your heart, and what is God speaking to you?

3. What changes do you see happening in your life?

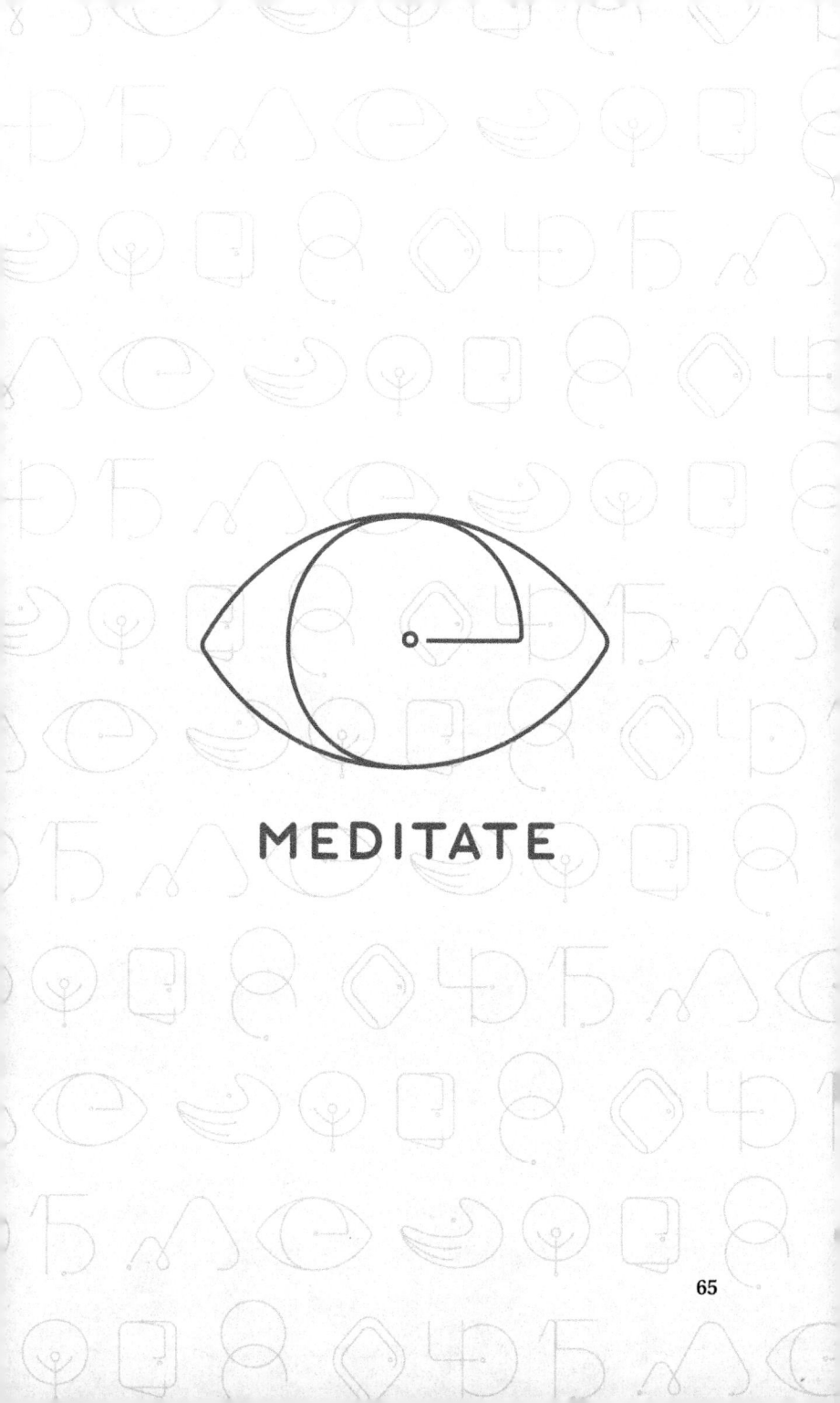

MEDITATE

MEDITATE

Reflect on the Scriptures and let the Holy Spirit apply them to your life.

May the words of my mouth and the meditation of my heart be pleasing to you, O LORD, my rock and my redeemer (Psalm 19:14).

"There was something so amazing about waking up every morning and giving myself time to put God first, to think about Him; how wonderful He is, how awesome. Just those single moments had a huge impact on the outcome of my day. My day was filled with a new sense of peace and His presence, no matter what I did."

That was how a young lady named Ana summed up her experience with the 40-Day Worship Experience. She discovered the importance of setting her thoughts on God, rather than allowing herself to be distracted and dismayed by the influences around her.

Every minute of every day, an intense battle wages around us. It's an unseen, spiritual battle between good and evil (Ephesians 2:2–3). The battle is over the mind. War is waged continually for control of our thoughts on multiple fronts.

We are active participants in the battle, not just spectators. Abraham, Moses, David, and Jesus and His disciples all faced this struggle, and through the grace of Jesus, we can be as victorious as they were.

The key to maintaining correct thoughts is to allow God's Word to transform you by the renewing of your mind. Romans 12:2 says, "Don't copy the behavior and customs of this world, but let God transform you into a new person by changing the way you think. Then you will learn to know God's will for you, which is good and pleasing and perfect."

Our inner thoughts must be renewed. The Bible is the inspired Word of God and is sufficient to guard and guide our mind in every area (2 Timothy 3:16). We must learn to think according to the Word: pure, wholesome, faith-filled thoughts (Philippians 4:8).

> THE KEY TO MAINTAINING CORRECT THOUGHTS IS TO ALLOW GOD'S WORD TO TRANSFORM YOU BY THE RENEWING OF YOUR MIND.

Regular meditation on the Word is a crucial component to the 40-Day Worship Experience. After you have deliberately surrendered yourself to God, and after you start the flow of the Spirit by celebrating His goodness to you, take time to meditate on His Word and be renewed in your mind.

To "meditate," in the biblical sense of the word, means to focus our mind on a particular truth and allow it to speak to us. It is not emptying our mind of all thoughts, nor is it some sort of relaxation or centering technique. When we meditate on God's Word, we intentionally digest what we are reading. We ponder a particular truth or passage, evaluate it, interact with it, submit to it, and apply it to our life.

Meditating is different than simply reading. We read for information, but we meditate for transformation. Think about what you read until it begins to affect your day-to-day existence. It must become personal—a word from God spoken directly to you.

Psalms 1:2-3 describes the health and vitality that those who meditate on God's Word experience: "They delight in the law of the Lord, meditating on it day and night. They are like trees planted along the riverbank, bearing fruit each season. Their leaves never wither, and they prosper in all they do."

> WE READ FOR INFORMATION, BUT WE MEDITATE FOR TRANSFORMATION.

Mind Matters

Whoever controls our mind controls our entire life. Proverbs 23:7 tells us, "As [a man] thinks in His heart, so is he" (NKJV). The root Hebrew word for "think" means a "gate" or "opening" (Strong's). It refers to a place of entry. Both good and evil enter our lives through the gateway of our mind.

The mind has always been the main battlefield, beginning in the Garden of Eden when Satan lied to Eve about the tree of the knowledge of good and evil (Genesis 3:1–5). Satan attacked her through her thoughts, trying to get her to view the tree and its fruit as something other than what they were.

Satan's attack began with words which did not line up with the words of God. He directed lies at the gate of Eve's mind. She had a choice about which thoughts to let in and which thoughts to keep out. Eve decided to agree with thoughts that were contrary to what God had said.

This is the first step of deception. Never underestimate the power of a thought. Satan's most potent weapon is his ability to deceive. He uses lies that lead us to wrong conclusions about God, ourselves, others, our purpose in life, and any other area that would draw us away from God. We must learn to become excellent gatekeepers, discerning and choosing what we let into our minds.

Where do thoughts go after they are allowed to pass through our mental gate? In Luke 8, Jesus tells the parable of the sower. He likens the heart to a garden and the condition of the heart to soil. Depending on the state of the soil, the seed—which represents the Word of God—either dies or flourishes.

He describes four types of soil. Three of them are not conducive to good growth: the hard ground, the rocky ground, and the thorn-filled ground. Only the last one—good ground, representing a pure heart—

> THE THOUGHTS WE ALLOW THROUGH THE GATEWAY OF OUR MIND DETERMINE THE CONDITION OF OUR HEART.

is able to receive the seed of God's Word and produce a bountiful crop.

Jesus is saying that what we allow into our heart affects the condition of our soul and thus its capacity to produce a healthy life. The seed was the same in all cases. It was good, and it had the power to bring about healthy growth. But the hearer's heart condition made all the difference.

In Greek, the word "heart" is *kardia*. It refers to the place we think, feel, and decide. The thoughts we allow through the gateway of our mind determine the condition of our heart. This is why what we allow ourselves to think about is so critical.

Our heart is where we mix the thoughts we have allowed through the gate of our mind. It is where we develop attitudes and beliefs about God, life, our circumstances, and ourselves. These attitudes and beliefs drive our actions. Our actions, therefore, are the outcome of thoughts and feelings that we previously allowed into our heart.

Meditate | 71

Jesus told His disciples, "A good person produces good things from the treasury of a good heart, and an evil person produces evil things from the treasury of an evil heart. What you say flows from what is in your heart" (Luke 6:45). The NKJV renders the final phrase, "Out of the abundance of the heart his mouth speaks."

You can see how everything goes back to the source of our thoughts and how critical it is that we learn to take every thought captive to the obedience of Christ. Listen to what Paul says in 2 Corinthians 10:3–5 (NIV).

> For though we live in the world, we do not wage war as the world does. The weapons we fight with are not the weapons of the world. On the contrary, they have divine power to demolish strongholds. We demolish arguments and every pretension that sets itself up against the knowledge of God, and we take captive every thought to make it obedient to Christ.

Thinking about Thinking

One of the reasons we allow destructive thought patterns to continue unchecked is because we don't take the time to think about what we think about.

Take a quick mental inventory. How is your thought life? What is having the greatest influence on your mental state? Is it worry and fear, or is it faith and trust? Are you able to control your thoughts, or do your thoughts control you? Our thoughts are influenced by many things. We must be aware of this so we can proactively cultivate a healthy heart and mind.

The most obvious influence on our thoughts is *our immediate environment*, which we perceive through our five senses. The things we see, hear, touch, smell, and taste can have either a positive or negative impact on our mental condition. We must become effective at guarding our senses.

Our flesh also influences our thoughts. I am not referring to our physical flesh, but rather to our fallen nature. The flesh is self-centered at the core. It will do nothing but lead us into bondage and heartache. Be cautious of that inner voice that is capable of creating thoughts leading to destruction.

The internal war we feel is very real. Galatians 5:16–18 explains this battle in detail:

> So I say, let the Holy Spirit guide your lives. Then you won't be doing what your sinful nature craves. The sinful nature wants to do evil, which is just the opposite of what the Spirit wants. And the Spirit gives us desires that are the opposite of what the sinful nature desires. These two forces are constantly fighting each other, so you are not free to carry out your good intentions. But when you are directed by the Spirit, you are not under obligation to the law of Moses.

The process of our fallen nature being tempted into doing evil always involves internal thoughts, values, and predispositions. James 1:14–15 states, "Temptation comes from our own desires, which entice us and drag us away. These desires give birth to sinful actions. And when sin is allowed to grow, it gives birth to death."

The battle can feel exhausting at times, and to be honest, it will not go away fully until we are united with our Lord in Heaven. But we can be victorious in every battle through the grace of Jesus. The more we meditate on Him and His Word, the more the flesh loses its hold on us.

Besides our environment and our own flesh, *our thoughts* can also be affected by the spiritual world. Both the Holy Spirit and demonic spirits can influence us, depending on whose voice we listen to and how we respond.

We see this illustrated in Acts 5, when Ananias and his wife Sapphira attempted to lie about their giving to the church. Peter directly references the influence of Satan on their minds: "Ananias, why have you let Satan fill your heart? You lied to the Holy Spirit, and you kept some of the money for yourself" (verse 3).

> WE CAN BE VICTORIOUS IN EVERY BATTLE THROUGH THE GRACE OF JESUS.

The Bible calls Satan the tempter. He has the capacity to influence our thoughts in an attempt to deceive us into doing what opposes God's will for us. That doesn't mean we are obligated to give in to those thoughts, of course. When we realize they come from a diabolical source, we must choose to reject them and fill our minds with godly thoughts.

In summary, everything around us in both the seen world and the unseen world is exerting influence on our thoughts and competing for that inner place called the heart. Our task is to identify the source of our thoughts and ensure that we are meditating on healthy, godly things. Philippians 4:8 says, "Fix your thoughts on what is true, and honorable, and right, and pure, and lovely, and admirable. Think about things that are excellent and worthy of praise."

Gatekeepers

We have seen that our thoughts are not idle or passive. Whether we realize it or not, they are always at work, influencing and shaping our lives.

The heart is a fertile place, and the thoughts that we allow to take root in our heart germinate into attitudes, actions, and ultimately our destiny.

We are called to be the gatekeepers of our own heart. Proverbs 4:23 says, "Guard your heart above all else, for it determines the course of your life." Each of us must learn how to become an excellent gatekeeper, taking every thought captive.

To be successful gatekeepers, it is imperative that we read and meditate on the Word of God daily. This is the key to a transformed mind. David said, "I have hidden your word in my heart, that I might not sin against you" (Psalm 119:11).

The Word of God is living and active. It will enter our heart as seed and grow up into the truths of who God is, how much He loves us, what His purpose is for our lives, and how to think and behave. Hebrews 4:12 says, "The word of God is alive and powerful. It is sharper than the sharpest two-edged sword, cutting between soul and spirit, between joint and marrow. It exposes our innermost thoughts and desires."

God's Word is a light for our feet on a dark path (Psalm 119:105). The world is a dark place: incorrect thoughts and attitudes can easily trip us up. God's truth illuminates our way, exposing error and pointing us on the path to success.

The Word of God is a love letter to us. Our human tendency is to doubt God's love because we are acutely aware of our failures. God's thoughts toward us are written in His Word, and He wants to plant all those good thoughts in our hearts.

Have a heart that is hungry to hear from God. Make a plan, and begin reading the Word daily as part of your devotional time. For the next forty days, as you come to the Lord with a surrendered life, using music to celebrate your walk with Him, you will find your heart open and receptive to the Word of God. This is a great time to meditate on the Scriptures.

Begin reading the section you have chosen for the day. Ask the Holy Spirit to help you understand what you are reading. The Spirit has been sent to help you hear what the Word of God says and to apply it. Don't be afraid to ask for His aid. The Bible tells us to ask, seek, and knock (Matthew 7:7).

Let the Holy Spirit speak to you through the passage, and meditate on what He says. Let the thoughts of His Word mingle with your thoughts. Allow God to do a work inside you. Do not be frustrated if you don't understand everything you are reading—just continue to read and meditate on His Word daily, and trust the Holy Spirit to reveal what you need to know.

Through meditation on God's Word, we have a greater awareness of His presence. His Word is who He is. As we interact with it, we interact with Jesus Himself (John 1:1-4).

The Holy Spirit and His Word will expose wrong attitudes and beliefs. The Bible calls these things strongholds or false arguments (2 Corinthians 10:3-5). Each of us have them, but as we give ourselves to reading and meditating on God's Word, our mind and heart are purified.

> GOD'S THOUGHTS TOWARD US ARE WRITTEN IN HIS WORD, AND HE WANTS TO PLANT ALL THOSE GOOD THOUGHTS IN OUR HEARTS.

Keep in mind that you may experience some

resistance to getting started. This happens because there is a battle over your life. The enemy does not want you to get started. Don't let that discourage you.

How should you begin? In the Journal section at the end of this book, you will find suggested passages for the first forty days. This would be a good starting point. If you are on a different reading plan, or if you use a daily devotional with Scriptures in it, you can follow that instead. Over the years, I have used several different plans to read and meditate on God's Word.

> RELAX AND ENJOY THE JOURNEY.

The point is to get started and to meditate on the Word each morning. Relax and enjoy the journey. You aren't trying to get through large quantities of Scripture in each sitting—you might spend the whole time on one passage or even on one phrase.

As you are reading in the atmosphere of the flow of God's presence, you will at times sense an inner stirring about certain passages of Scripture. This is God speaking to you, revealing Himself through His written Word.

One day, shortly after Jesus' resurrection, He spent several hours walking and talking with two men on the road to Emmaus (Luke 24:34–49). They didn't recognize Him, but they were astounded at how He made the Word come alive. Later, they described it this way: "Didn't our hearts burn within us as he talked with us on the road and explained the Scriptures to us?" (verse 32).

This is what the Holy Spirit does for us when we take

time to read and meditate on the Word of God.

Use your journal to write the Scriptures and thoughts that are inspiring to you. This is God speaking to you through His Word. You will want to remember what you are reading and studying so you can reflect on it later.

As you discipline yourself to read God's Word every morning, it will plant seed in your heart that in time will grow into a beautiful garden of truth. You may not realize at the time the powerful effect it is having, but as you enjoy God's presence and take time to surrender, celebrate, and meditate, His life will begin to flow out of your heart.

You will find that the meditation aspect of your prayer time continues through the day. The way you think will change. You will be more aware of God's thoughts. You will identify erroneous mindsets and incorrect attitudes more quickly. You will find yourself applying practically what God spoke to you in the morning.

Meditation is thinking about something over and over again. The idiom "chewing's one's cud" or "chewing on something for awhile" is essentially the idea of meditating. Cows and other animals chew their cud by bringing food back into their mouth and chewing it, often for hours, until it is able to be properly digested.

We "chew the cud" of the Word by bringing it to mind repeatedly, extracting everything we can from it and digesting its meaning. The Word of God is food to our heart, like natural food to our body, and what we ingest ultimately becomes part of who we are.

The Word will interact with our thoughts, feelings,

attitudes, beliefs, and habits. Some of these will be in contradiction to the Word of God and will need to be removed. This is part of the transformation process, and it occurs naturally as the spirit of our mind is renewed (Ephesians 4:23).

The beautiful thing about the sanctification process is that we don't have to grit our teeth and make it happen. It is a result of grace and the power of the Holy Spirit at work in us. As we meditate on God's truths, we become like Him. Our thoughts change, then our attitudes and emotions, then our actions. Our responsibility in this process is to let it happen. It's that simple. We cooperate with the Holy Spirit as He gently leads us into paths of righteousness, peace, and joy.

Of course, this is not always a comfortable process. Reading the Bible from an academic or intellectual standpoint is much easier than opening our mind, will, and emotions to the scrutiny of the Spirit. When the Word of God suddenly becomes personal, when God speaks directly to a particular attitude or situation, we often feel simultaneously at peace and in conflict. We are at peace because we know God has spoken to us, but there is an internal conflict of the will and the emotions as we are confronted with the need to change.

Don't overreact to these emotions. Remind yourself that you *want* to change. Remember that you have surrendered yourself to a good God who desires only good things for you. Then humbly meditate on what God is showing you and ask for His help to make needed adjustments.

Earlier, I mentioned the three enemies that are competing for access to our heart: the flesh, the devil, and the world system. The Word is an effective weapon to defeat all three of these enemies. "And you will know the truth, and the truth will set you free" (John 8:32). Jesus Himself used the Word to defeat temptation in the wilderness (Matthew 4:1-11).

King David said, "Search me, O God, and know my heart; test me and know my anxious thoughts. Point out anything in me that offends you, and lead me along the path of everlasting life" (Psalm 139:23-24). He understood the power of wrong thoughts because he saw what happened when a lustful thought on a rooftop was not brought into check. That thought led him down a path of sorrow, sin, violence, and pain—he committed adultery with a married woman, Bathsheba, and then had her husband murdered (2 Samuel 11).

> AS WE MEDITATE ON GOD'S TRUTHS, WE BECOME LIKE HIM.

We can only think one thing at a time: not more, not less. That means that the best way to combat negative thoughts isn't to try to stop thinking about them, but to think about something else instead: God's Word.

We have authority over every thought that tries to enter our heart through our mind. Each thought is evaluated and filtered by the Word and the Spirit. All this happens in a nanosecond inside our being. If we determine the thought is of God, it can be allowed in. If not, then we take it captive and expel it from our mind. The phrase in 2 Corinthians 10:3–5, "take captive every thought to make it obedient to Christ," is a military concept that refers to seizing and removing the thought by force.

Often people believe they cannot control a thought or attitude, but this simply is not true. We always have a choice, and we have the power of God residing within us through the Holy Spirit to make the right one.

As we become more aware of our own thoughts, this process of taking every thought captive will become easier. I have heard it said that the best way for bank employees to learn to recognize counterfeit money is by spending hours and hours with real money. When they encounter a false bill, they recognize it immediately because they are so familiar with authentic bills. This same principle holds true with our thoughts. The more familiar we get with the truths in God's Word, the more easily we detect error.

As you read and meditate on the Word of God daily, new life will enter your soul. You will defeat temptation more easily, you will have new self-control in your attitudes and actions, and you will be more aware of God's presence than ever.

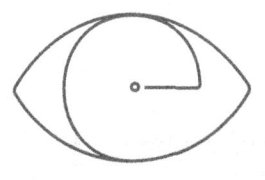

MEDITATE

Chapter Summary

During the 40-Day Worship Experience, you are reading your Bible every day. You might be reading the portion of Psalms provided in the Journal section or other portions of Scripture. As you read, I encourage you to open your heart up to God's Word and learn to meditate on what He is saying to you.

Meditation, in the biblical sense of the term, is a constant rethinking about the Word. Don't rush through your reading. Don't be in a hurry to finish large portions of Scripture. One morning you might read entire chapters, and another morning you might spend the whole time digesting one phrase or verse.

Jesus said, "People do not live by bread alone, but by every word that comes from the mouth of God" (Matthew 4:4). The Word of God will speak to our heart and give us clear direction for life. Never underestimate the power of the seed of His Word being planted in your heart.

Discussion Questions

Take a few moments to pray this prayer, then answer the following questions.

"Jesus, You are the Word of God that is a light for my feet. I pray that You would illuminate Your Word in my heart, transforming and changing me from the inside out. I pray that Your thoughts would become my thoughts and that I would not sin against You with my thoughts, attitudes, or actions. I am excited to learn Your ways and walk on Your path. I pray Your Word will transform my heart today."

1. How important is it to get the Word of God planted in your heart? What are some hindrances you have faced to reading the Bible daily?

2. Read Psalms 119:11 aloud. What does this verse mean to you?

    I have hidden your word in my heart,
    that I might not sin against you. (Psalm 119:11)

3. Read Luke 8:4-15. What does this passage tell you about your heart? What is your heart compared to?

4. Picture your heart as a garden. Who are the "enemies" of your heart, and how do they gain access? How can the Word of God defeat those enemies?

Your Mornings So Far

1. What are some challenges you've faced during the 40-Day Worship Experience?

2. What is happening in your heart, and what is God speaking to you?

3. What changes do you see happening in your life?

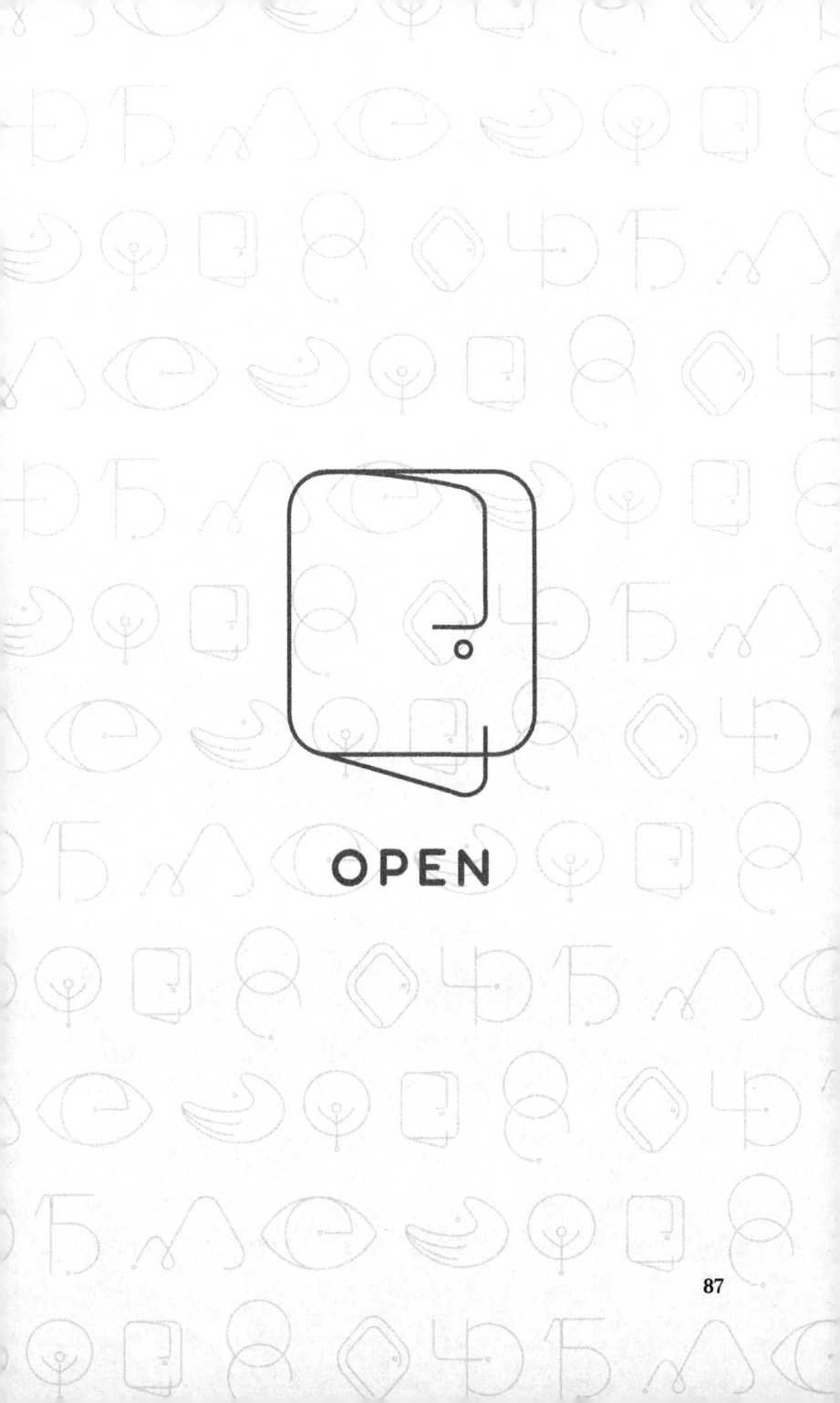

OPEN

OPEN

**Allow the Holy Spirit to bring healing
and change to specific areas of your life.**

Look! I stand at the door and knock. If you hear my voice and open the door, I will come in, and we will share a meal together as friends (Revelation 3:20).

It's ironic that in the areas where we need help the most, we often close ourselves off from honest dialogue with our Savior. He created us and knows every detail of our lives better than we do, yet we seem to think we can hide things from Him. It's far better to open our heart to His searching and direction.

One person who took my prayer class, a man named James, summed up his experience this way: "The last forty days have been a very interesting time. I have both enjoyed and completely disliked what I have gone through. The part that I enjoyed was the connection with the Father that got me through the day with a quite awesome outlook. The part I disliked was when

God brought to my attention things that need to change in my life."

I couldn't have said it better! But it is this openness to the direction and correction of the Holy Spirit that makes our relationship with Him authentic.

Enjoying God's continual presence in our life requires that no area be excluded from the light of His Word and His amazing love for us. We must not allow our lives to become compartmentalized, giving God access to some areas but not to others.

Earlier, I discussed approaching God in surrender. "Surrender" refers to an overarching heart attitude of submission to God. The term "open," as used in this chapter, is more specific. I am referring to honest dialogue with God regarding every area. Once we have spent time each morning in surrender, celebration, and meditation, our heart is prepared to come boldly before the Lord and to hear what He has to say about anything He chooses to address.

> EVERYTHING WE ARE, EVERYTHING WE HAVE, AND EVERYTHING WE WILL EVER BE BELONGS TO HIM.

When we surrender our will to His will, we recognize our life is not our own. Everything we are, everything we have, and everything we will ever be belongs to Him. He has the right to address and direct every facet of our existence.

Hide No More

The idea of giving God complete access made me uncomfortable at first, and it will probably have the same effect on you. Why? Because often, when we draw close to God, we are ashamed of who we are and what we have done.

Before the fall, Adam and Eve were naked and unashamed before God. In a spiritual sense, this is how we are meant to live under the New Covenant. We are to be spiritually "naked," or transparent, in our hearts and minds. If not, carnal areas will continue to manifest and find a negative outlet, hindering our closeness to Him and our progress in life.

When Adam and Eve sinned, they introduced guilt and shame to the human race. They hid from God—the only one who could really help them. Their sin, together with the resulting guilt and shame, separated them from their Creator (Genesis 3).

These two feelings—guilt and shame—continue to be an issue for all of us. They often keep us from opening up fully to God and receiving the grace we need.

Guilt is a sense of responsibility for having committed some wrongdoing. Guilt is not necessarily wrong. It is meant to motivate us toward repentance, change, and restitution, however, not to become a lifestyle. Shame goes one step further than guilt, referring to a pervading sense of emotional distress and disgrace.

Both feelings are rooted in one thing: our sins, whether real or imagined. We are painfully aware of our shortcomings. When we see the glory and perfection of God, our natural reaction is to try to hide our filthy, shameful behavior from His view.

We must realize that in redemption, the blood of Jesus blotted out our sins. They are no longer visible (Psalm 103:12). When God sees us, He sees only the pure holiness of Jesus. That means our guilt and our shame have been removed as well. Jesus took those things upon Himself when He died upon the cross. There is no need for us to continually rehearse our wrong acts or focus on our failures.

The first step to openness with God is realizing that sin no longer separates us. God is not mad at us. He is not frustrated or disappointed with us. Our repeated failures don't surprise Him—He knows us better than we know ourselves, yet He still loves us. He longs to assure us of His forgiveness. He is proud of us and our efforts to do the right thing, like an earthly father and mother are proud of their children.

> But God showed his great love for us by sending Christ to die for us while we were still sinners. And since we have been made right in God's sight by the blood of Christ, he will certainly save us from God's condemnation. For since our friendship with God was restored by the death of his Son while we were still his enemies, we will certainly be saved through the life of his Son. So now we can rejoice in our wonderful new relationship

with God because our Lord Jesus Christ has made us friends of God. (Romans 5:8-11)

It's time to come out of hiding. Our sin is not the problem any longer—it's guilt and shame that prolong the separation. Don't allow fear or embarrassment to keep you from God, the very one who can heal your wounds and give you grace to rise again.

Open for Healing

If we are honest with ourselves, we know that we need help to live a pure life. Good news! God doesn't expect us to do that on our own. As I just mentioned, His grace took care of our guilt and shame. Now, His grace will also help us live differently than before.

We must realize that this is a process. The Bible calls this process sanctification, a term that refers to becoming holy or setting ourselves apart from sin and the world's way of living. This process will last our whole lives, and while it requires hard choices at times, the rewards are great. Sin is enjoyable for a moment, but it does nothing but destroy us and those we love. God wants to set us free from the things that are holding us back so we can truly enjoy the life He has given us.

Sanctification requires that we be open, honest, and transparent before God. This includes both external areas like actions and decisions as well as internal ones like thoughts and emotions. These are connected, as I described earlier: thoughts become attitudes and beliefs, and attitudes and beliefs become actions. We need to come to the point where we naturally and easily open each area to God's evaluation, especially our innermost thoughts and feelings.

The book of Psalms shows us that David was able to express His true feelings to God. We need to practice this type of honesty with our Heavenly Father by expressing what is really going on inside our heart. He isn't going to be angry with us for being honest. More than anyone else, God can handle our feelings and thoughts. Honesty is the first step toward healing and help.

> MORE THAN ANYONE ELSE, GOD CAN HANDLE OUR FEELINGS AND THOUGHTS.

Human emotions are fickle and can lead us astray if we are not careful. Not everything we feel is accurate. The devil is crafty, and he tries to manipulate the things we face in life to create discouragement, disillusionment, hurt, bitterness, and resentment. We can counter these attempts of the enemy to deceive us by having open communication with God. When difficult, confusing, or disturbing thoughts or experiences come our way, we must be able to go to the Lord in heartfelt conversation.

"Heartfelt conversation" does not mean disrespect or accusation. There is a difference between going to God with questions and questioning God. The first is done in honesty and humility, recognizing that God is in charge; the second means attributing wrong motives to God and challenging His goodness.

Remember, Isaiah tells us God's ways are higher that our ways and His thoughts than our thoughts (Isaiah 55:9). Life does not always make sense intellectually, so our feelings can get out of line. Fears assail our mind and heart. Condemnation, guilt, and shame pile up.

It is in these moments that we most need to get alone with God and let our heart connect to His. Sitting in our "worry chair," as I did, and fretting over everything is futile. But God is never overwhelmed, and He is waiting for us to run into His arms (Proverbs 18:10). He wants to help us keep our circumstances from dictating our thoughts, feeling, and actions. This is what we gain when we open our heart to Him. Our response to every situation should come out of the leading of the Holy Spirit.

Don't End Up in a Ditch

We've all heard stories about drivers who overreacted to something and ended up driving off the road. Maybe they spilled their coffee on their lap, or a squirrel ran across the road, or they drifted into loose gravel and overcorrected. The point is, a small problem became a much bigger one because of their exaggerated response.

Don't end up in a ditch just because you spilled your coffee. In other words, don't allow your emotions and thoughts to blow negative situations out of perspective. I know how this works—I was an expert at overreacting! As I mentioned earlier, I suffered from panic and anxiety for over thirty-eight years.

Emotional stability and freedom from fear are two of the greatest results I've seen in my own prayer and worship journey. As I spend time with God each morning, my emotions and perspective are continually brought into line with God's thoughts.

Once, during the season of David's life when he and his ragtag army were running from Saul, they returned from an expedition and found that their wives, children, and possessions had been taken by the Amalekites (1 Samuel 30). David and his "mighty men," as they were known, were shocked and heartbroken, to the point that the men talked of killing David.

David had lost his family as well, and he had no idea what to do. Instead of allowing his emotions to take over, though, he encouraged himself in the Lord (verse 6). David was brutally honest with God because he was in desperate need of help, an attitude we see throughout Psalms. David had a close walk with the Lord and a healthy understanding of who he was and who God was. As a result, David was able to find a realistic, godly perspective about a very negative situation.

He then asked God for direction about how to reclaim what the enemy had taken. God directed Him to fight back, and David and his men ended up winning a great victory and regaining what they had lost. We can only imagine what would have happened if David had overreacted emotionally.

Cultivating an open and honest heart before the Lord will short-circuit wrong thoughts and feelings in times of crisis. It will help us minimize negative reactions and make rational decisions.

Years ago, I had a friend going through a separation from his wife. Thoughts and feelings of pain and rejection were leading him in the wrong direction. One day, in desperation, he told me he just wanted to end his life. I told him I was not as concerned about his current situation as I was about the decision he was about to make in response.

> DON'T ALLOW YOUR EMOTIONS AND THOUGHTS TO BLOW NEGATIVE SITUATIONS OUT OF PERSPECTIVE.

Thankfully, he persevered in faith. Nine months later, he was reunited with his wife. Just think what could have happened had he overreacted to those negative thoughts in a time of crisis.

Our fallen human nature is very skilled at self-deception. In every situation, we must be honest with God and ourselves about how we are feeling and what we are thinking. Are we allowing self-pity, discouragement, anger, or other strong emotions to skew our judgment?

Jeremiah 17:9–10 says, "The human heart is the most deceitful of all things, and desperately wicked. Who really knows how bad it is? But I, the Lord, search all hearts and examine secret motives. I give all people their due rewards, according to what their actions deserve."

We can be under deception at any given moment. No one is immune: even great men and women of the Bible were deceived at times. The problem with deception is that we are blind to it. That's where humility and openness come in. We give the Holy Spirit access and permission to bring correction to any area He sees fit.

In Genesis chapter 4, we read a conversation between God and Cain, after God had rejected Cain's offering. Cain was angry, and he was probably already plotting the death of his brother. God could see that Satan was crouching at the door of Cain's heart. God warned him that evil was lurking in his heart and that he needed to be honest about what was going on inside. He had to overcome the evil and do what was right.

> NOW IS THE TIME TO APPROACH THE THRONE OF GRACE.

This is a clear picture of how sin can get a foothold (Ephesians 4:27). It starts small, with an unchecked wrong attitude, but it has the potential to grow into a great mistake.

Though Cain engaged in dialogue with God, he did not open every area of his heart and receive the help God offered. Instead, he responded out of his hurt, which resulted in the murder of his brother and his own banishment.

All of us face difficult circumstances, offenses, and temptation. We cannot afford to compartmentalize our thoughts and feelings. We need to learn to go to God first, and to do so with transparency and authenticity. The 40-Day Worship Experience places us in a position to talk to God first, every day, about anything we are facing. As His grace and wisdom flow through us, we will make sound decisions.

What areas in your life need to be opened up to God? Are there any anger or lust issues? Do you struggle with depression? Has fear had a grip on your heart recently? Are there parts of your life where you would like to see change? Are there things you are embarrassed to open up to the Lord about? Now is the time to approach the throne of grace. There is no shame or condemnation—only God's supernatural power to achieve victory.

The Surrender Prayer, found toward the end of this book, just before the Journal, can be a helpful tool to walk you through different heart issues that need to be given over to God.

OPEN

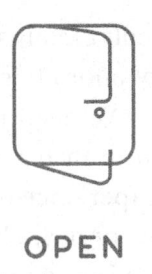

Chapter Summary

This chapter discusses opening our inner world up to the Lord and inviting Him in. In Revelation 3:20, Jesus says that He stands at the door and knocks. He is referring to the door of our heart. Jesus wants to be able to visit every room in our heart. We have access to Him, and He wants complete access to us.

Opening our heart fully can be frightening if we feel like we have something to hide. We try to compartmentalize it: we grant Jesus access to part of it but not to the whole thing. In reality, of course, God already sees everything. He knows our thoughts before we think them. Just because we don't admit a weakness to God doesn't mean it is hidden from Him. It is far better to give Him free access and trust that He has our best interests in mind.

Often, guilt and shame will keep us from going to the door and letting Jesus meet with us. This happened first in the garden after Adam and Eve sinned. They ended up trying to hide from God. God came looking for them, found them, and called to them (Genesis 3:8-11).

Jesus wants to have fellowship with us. He doesn't come to judge us or condemn us, but to love us and show us how to live in victory and peace. God's love is always knocking. It's our challenge to hear the knock and respond by inviting Him in. It's time to let God do a deeper work. No more hiding. Don't be afraid. Your healing is now!

Discussion Questions

Take a few moments to pray this prayer, then answer the following questions.

"Lord Jesus, just as David prayed, I ask You to search my heart and see if anything in me displeases You. I don't want to compartmentalize my heart anymore. Instead, I am inviting You into every area of my life. I don't want to hide anything from You. I admit this makes me nervous, but I'm trusting You to do a deep work of grace within me. I am excited to let You love me in a fresh, new way and to reveal the areas where I need healing and transformation."

1. Is it hard for you to be vulnerable and transparent about your weaknesses and failures? Why or why not?

2. Read Psalm 139:23-24 aloud. What does this passage mean to you?

   Search me, O God, and know my heart;
   test me and know my anxious thoughts.
   Point out anything in me that offends you,
   and lead me along the path of everlasting life.
   (Psalm 139:23-24)

3. Read Colossians 3:1–5 (NLT). What do these verses tell you about the deceptive nature of sin that is still within us? Can you think of areas where sin could be "lurking" in your own life?

   Since you have been raised to new life with Christ, set your sights on the realities of heaven, where Christ sits in the place of honor at God's right hand. Think about the things of heaven, not the things of earth. For you died to this life, and your real life is hidden with Christ in God. And when Christ, who is your life, is revealed to the whole world, you will share in all his glory.

   So put to death the sinful, earthly things lurking within you. Have nothing to do with sexual immorality, impurity, lust, and evil desires. Don't be greedy, for a greedy person is an idolater, worshiping the things of this world. (Colossians 3:1-5)

4. Are there any specific areas of struggle you're facing that you would like to mention?

Your Mornings So Far

1. What are some challenges you've faced during the 40-Day Worship Experience?

2. What is happening in your heart, and what is God speaking to you?

3. What changes do you see happening in your life?

DEDICATE

DEDICATE

Commit your day to God's use and ask for His help.

The Lord directs the steps of the godly. He delights in every detail of their lives. Though they stumble, they will never fall, for the Lord holds them by the hand.
(Psalm 37:23-24)

The best part of life is the thrill of God's presence. Once you have truly experienced His presence, nothing else compares. Sensing His love, hearing His words of encouragement, relaxing in His peace that surpasses understanding—these are just a few of the treasures we find when we spend time with Him. As David said, "You will show me the path of life; in your presence is fullness of joy; at your right hand are pleasures forevermore" (Psalm 16:11).

Once we realize His presence is all we really want or need, then the rest of life becomes an opportunity to experience Him. Even the hard times are just an opportunity for God to reveal Himself and for us to draw closer to

Him. Life takes on new meaning. Our focus shifts. We see God's hand in everything we do, and we become aware of His continual presence. Temporal things diminish in value, while eternal things increase.

This all-inclusive approach to life—seeing God at work and following Him in every facet of our existence—is the essence of our fifth principle, *dedicate*.

Down-to-Earth Worship

During this forty-day journey, we have discussed surrendering our life, celebrating God's goodness, meditating on His Word, and opening our heart to Him. Next, I encourage you to take a few moments to dedicate your day to His leading. If you are willing to do this, you will see God's favor and blessing in a new way.

Dedicating our mind, will, emotions, and actions to God is a practical expression of worship. It's relatively easy to tell God how wonderful He is, but as we all know, attitudes and actions speak louder than words. We have truly become worshippers when we desire to please Him in every aspect of our lives.

Dedication begins on the inside, with a surrendered, humble, and faith-filled heart. It quickly spills over into the physical world through our words and actions. It's the practical outworking of our inner, spiritual life dedicated to following Him.

Dedication flows out of a daily decision to give God complete control of our lives. ~~Trust Him, lean on Him, and learn from Him~~. There is a learning curve here: it's hard at first, but it gets easier with practice. Soon,

> WE HAVE TRULY BECOME WORSHIPPERS WHEN WE DESIRE TO PLEASE HIM IN EVERY ASPECT OF OUR LIVES.

stewarding or managing all God gives us through His grace and favor will be our heart's desire.

In our relationship with God, <u>the level of intimacy is directly related to our level of dedication</u>. God delights in a surrendered heart. A teachable, humble, trusting attitude opens us up to a flow of blessings we could not imagine.

Genesis 6:9 describes the lifestyle of Noah, a great hero of faith, this way: "Noah was a righteous man, the only blameless person living on earth at the time, and he walked in close fellowship with God." Everything Noah did was an act of worship to God, and he walked in true relationship with Him. We can have that same relationship!

Where Transformation Happens

Often, we attempt to earn God's favor through good works done in our own strength without fully submitting our will. This backfires because, until our will is given over to Him, we will continue to live according to the flesh, no matter how hard we try.

The book of Galatians tells us, "Let the Holy Spirit guide your lives. Then you won't be doing what your sinful nature craves" (5:16). The opposite is also true: if we do not follow the Spirit, we will default to fleshly desires.

God wants our heart first, even before our actions. Jesus already paid for our sins, and God knows that if our heart is right, our actions will follow. He can work with a soft heart.

Desiring to follow God in everything I do has been a key to finding personal freedom. As I've mentioned, fear is my biggest enemy, and depression is a close second. I found that God is not intimidated by my problems or anxious about my future. When I give my life completely to Him, there is nothing left for me to worry or fret about. It's the most freeing feeling imaginable.

You'll Need a Bigger Box

Often we mentally separate our spiritual life from other, more "natural" pursuits. We put God in a little box: a few minutes each morning, maybe some quick prayers during the week, and church on Sunday.

God doesn't fit in our little box, however. That is not even realistic. He is everywhere, all the time. We can't compartmentalize our relationship with God, limiting

Him to certain times and places.

Every facet of our life is meant to revolve around Him. Every detail—no matter how "spiritual" or "practical"—is fulfilling the purpose of God on the earth. That includes family, vocation, ministry, health, and finances. Colossians 3:23 says, "Work willingly at everything you do, as though you were working for the Lord rather than for people."

As a believer, God lives inside of you and wants to be intimately involved in every detail and decision. He doesn't want to be Lord of your prayer time and just an afterthought for the rest of the day. He wants your full focus to be on Him.

Success Starts Here

God desires intimate involvement because He wants you to succeed. He wants to guide your steps and lead you into a place of peace and fulfillment. He wants to deliver you from the evil one and open up doors of opportunity for you. He wants to reveal Himself to you. He wants to give you the wisdom you need in every situation. He wants to show you all that He has for you and shower you with favor. The Bible says in Proverbs 16:3, "Commit your actions to the Lord, and your plans will succeed."

We are managers of the resources God has entrusted to us, and we are responsible for the course of our life. That is why we need God's help in all we do. Proverbs

3:5–6 says, "Trust in the Lord with all your heart; do not depend on your own understanding. Seek his will in all you do, and he will show you which path to take."

This is a famous passage of Scripture, and for good reason. So often, we just blast off into life and try our hardest to make things work out, but we don't stop long enough to involve God in the details. God longs to be present in every part of our life.

One person who took the 40-Day Worship Experience, a young lady named Erika, wrote this: "God has ceased to be something I call upon only when I need Him, He is now the one I walk with, side by side, as I do absolutely everything . . . Starting each day with this vital connection has increased my hunger and intimacy with my Savior. He is my lifeline, my source."

Often, people only remember to involve God during tragic or difficult moments. In those times, they suddenly recognize their need to look to a source outside themselves. While God is gracious and delights in helping us, if we seek Him only when we need to be rescued, we are missing the many wonderful moments we could spend with Him during non-emergencies. We lose out on the benefit of His wisdom, creative ideas, and proactive direction.

> YOUR TIME ALONE WITH HIM IN THE MORNING IS A LAUNCHPAD TO A DAY SPENT IMMERSED IN HIS PRESENCE.

When God created you, He envisioned continual friendship. He designed you with a need to share your life with others, and that starts with sharing your life with Him. Don't wait until your plans come crashing down to ask for help—create your strategies and build your future based on constant communion with the Lord.

This ongoing interaction with God was one of the things that stood out the most to Elizabeth, another student in my prayer class. She wrote at the end of her experience: "I spent more of the day in communication with God. I never realized beforehand how little I spoke with God throughout the day. When I was starting and ending my day with Him, it was easy to spend the rest of it with Him, too."

For the next forty days, I encourage you to consciously and deliberately dedicate everything you do to God. Start by opening up a continual dialogue with the Holy Spirit, and expect Him to guide you throughout the day. Your time alone with Him in the morning is a launchpad to a day spent immersed in His presence.

By the way, there is nothing "spooky" about letting the Holy Spirit direct your steps. I'm not talking about waiting for a voice from heaven to tell you what outfit to put on each morning or for an angel to cook your breakfast for you. While at times God may stop us in our tracks with a specific, clear, and nearly audible voice, He guides us first and foremost through His Word. The Bible shapes our integrity, values, wisdom, and conscience. Then the Holy Spirit makes the Word come alive in our day-to-day walk, applying the principles of the Word to each situation.

Being led by the Spirit means allowing Him to review our thoughts, words, and decisions and keep them aligned with the Word. It means staying alert to that inner sense of peace that indicates when we are living with a clear conscience in a manner that pleases God.

It isn't strange to carry on a dialogue with your Creator on a moment-to-moment basis. Start asking God questions throughout the day. Involve Him in the little things in your life. Imagine that He is right there with you—because He is.

I am convinced that God longs to experience the details of our life with us: the good and the bad, the frightening and the hilarious, the important and the trivial. Nothing is too small for Him to be involved, but we must invite Him in.

Lean and Let Go

Dedication starts with trusting God and learning how to lean on Him. Trust is a beautiful thing, but because of past experiences, many people find it difficult to fully trust anyone. They have learned the hard way that people can be fickle, selfish, and mean, and that everyone has to "look out for number one."

God, however, is not unfaithful and selfish, as humans so often are. He is totally trustworthy. He will never let us down. No matter what our experiences have been, we must learn to trust God wholeheartedly.

Isaiah 26:3 says, "You will keep Him in perfect peace, whose mind is stayed on you, because He trusts in you" (NKJV). The Hebrew word for "stayed" in this passage means "to lean on or upon; to prop; to take hold of" (Strong's). We must learn to lean on God. As we do, He will keep us in His perfect peace.

Paul encourages us in Philippians 4:6-7 to lean on God and let go of worry: "Don't worry about anything; instead, pray about everything. Tell God what you need, and thank Him for all He has done. Then you will experience God's peace, which exceeds anything we can understand. His peace will guard your hearts and minds as you live in Christ Jesus."

> IMAGINE THAT HE IS RIGHT THERE WITH YOU— BECAUSE HE IS.

Following God every moment of every day doesn't happen automatically, though. It takes intentionality. For the next forty days, as you enter each new day, pray a prayer of dedication to the Lord. Invite Him to lead and guide you. Ask Him to help you. You will find your heart becoming more aware of and sensitive to His presence.

Our goal is a growing interdependence on the Lord. This is not about getting God to help us do what we want; rather, it is discovering His beautiful plans for us and accomplishing them hand-in-hand with Him. It is walking in authentic fellowship with our heavenly Father as He fulfills His will in and through us. Remember, our lives are not our own anymore. We have surrendered them to Him.

If we look at our past, we can almost certainly remember decisions we have made where we did not involve the Lord's leading. Take an honest inventory: how did those choices work out for you? What was the long-term result of going down that path? Are there things you did your own way—in opposition to God's way—that you now recognize to be wrong decisions?

> IT'S TIME TO BURY THE WOULD-HAVES, COULD-HAVES, AND SHOULD-HAVES OF THE PAST.

This isn't meant to be an exercise in discouragement, just a simple reminder that we need God's involvement in our choices. Of course, His grace is so amazing that He is able to use even our mistakes to bring about blessing. He often guides us even when we are oblivious—or antagonistic—to His presence. But it is so much better to give Him complete access and free reign to lead us into peace and abundance.

Paul tells us in Philippians 3:13-14 to forget those things that are behind and press on to all the new things God has in store. It's time to bury the would-haves, could-haves, and should-haves of the past. From this day forward, resolve to invite the Lord to lead you in all you do.

Living with God leading the way is the most exciting adventure ever. We will never be alone again. We will never have the pressure of having to figure everything out on our own again.

There will be hard seasons, of course—life is not always easy. And we will face complex choices and difficult decisions. The difference is that we will be continually aware of God's presence and involvement. No matter what circumstances we face, we will know that God is at our side and that He is for us.

God has always been there for us—often we were just not aware of Him. When we dedicate the day to Him and seek His guidance, we hear differently and see differently. We become aware of His constant involvement in our day-to-day activities. He might be behind the scenes, but He never stops working on our behalf.

Instead of viewing certain situation as negative or terrifying, now we see the purpose of God in them. Where previously we might have reacted on our own and just aggravated the situation, now we are able to respond calmly and wisely.

Joseph, in the book of Genesis, exemplifies this trust in the Lord. When he was a young man, his brothers sold him into slavery out of jealousy. He was taken to Egypt as a slave, where he soon distinguished himself through his wisdom and effectiveness. But then he was falsely accused of attempting to rape his master's wife, and he was thrown in prison. In captivity, he again became respected for his wisdom and work ethic. He even

Dedicate | 117

interpreted the dreams of a fellow prisoner, who was subsequently released just as Joseph had predicted. The man promised to help Joseph when he got out, but he forgot. In time, God made a way for Joseph to be released, and within a short time, Pharaoh promoted him to second in command in all of Egypt.

It's hard to imagine a more up-and-down journey in life. Yet Joseph dedicated all he did to God, and he found favor even in the midst of difficult circumstances. Because of his close walk with God, he maintained his sensitive heart, sweet spirit, integrity, faith, and wisdom. Rather than reacting negatively, he continually found strength in God.

When he was reunited with his brothers and had it in his power to have his revenge, he said these famous words: "You intended to harm me, but God intended it all for good. He brought me to this position so I could save the lives of many people" (Genesis 50:20). His response demonstrated that he had kept his heart right through all the difficult years.

When we dedicate every moment to the Lord, we trust Him to guide our steps. Not all the things we go through will be pleasant in the moment, but we know this—God will be with us no matter what. Jesus' parting words when He ascended to heaven were, "Be sure of this: I am with you always, even to the end of the age" (Matthew 28:20). Tough situations are not a sign that God has abandoned us. On the contrary, they are an opportunity for us to lean even more heavily on Him.

Fear, anxiety, and stress are indicators that we are leaning on our own strength rather than trusting in God. For me, the most comforting Scripture in the book of Psalms is found in Psalm 46:1. "God is our refuge and strength, always ready to help in times of trouble." During the most difficult trial of my life, this truth became an anchor for my soul.

> GOD WILL BE WITH US NO MATTER WHAT.

Thousands of years ago, King Jehoshaphat, one of the kings of Israel, was facing an attack by three armies (2 Chronicles 20), and he was terrified. He looked to God for help, rather than leaning on his own logic or plans. God gave Him a clear strategy and delivered Him from his enemies.

God will do this for us as well. When we call on Him, He is always there. Proverbs 18:10 says, "The name of the Lord is a strong fortress, the godly run to him and are safe."

How do you react when you face impossible odds or unexpected resistance? Do you lean on God, or on your own ability or wisdom?

Over the next forty days, begin to build a habit of dedicating the little things, the big things, and all the things in between to God.

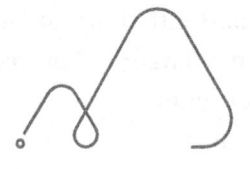

DEDICATE

Chapter Summary

If you are like me, it's all too easy to charge into the day without taking a minute to dedicate it to the Lord and ask for His help. The point of this chapter is to slow down, take a breath, and give your day over to God before it even starts.

As we all know, each day presents unique challenges, trials, adventures, and temptations. As you seek the Lord first, you begin to see how He is ordering your day. He already has a plan for you: you just need to discern His direction and climb on board.

People regularly tell me that the days they meet with the Lord go so much better than the days they don't. That doesn't mean that their time with the Lord keeps them from facing challenges; rather, it means they are better equipped to face those challenges.

Start each day with a prayer to dedicate all you do

to the Lord and to invite His help. Continue to dialogue with Him during the day. God is interested in every detail of your life. Know that God is with you every moment. Enjoy His closeness, relax in His strength, and live each day full of His abundant life.

Discussion Questions

Take a few moments to pray this prayer, then answer the following questions.

"Jesus, I dedicate this day to being with You. I am excited to walk with You into all You have for my life. I'm grateful You are using me to extend Your Kingdom. I pray that my eyes and ears will be open to what You are doing today. I am grateful that I can walk with You each day. Help me discern when I am not on Your path and direct my heart back to what You are doing. My passion is to know You and walk with you."

1. Have there been situations in the past when you didn't rely on the Lord's leading or ask for His help? How did they turn out?

2. Make a list of benefits that come from dedicating your day to God.

3. Read Proverbs 3:5-6. How is trust related to dedicating your day to the Lord? Share some challenges you have faced in trusting the Lord. Why is it sometimes difficult?

   Trust in the LORD with all your heart;
   do not depend on your own understanding.
   Seek his will in all you do,
   and he will show you which path to take.
   (Proverbs 3:5-6)

4. Read Psalm 37:23-24 aloud. What does this passage mean to you?

   The LORD directs the steps of the godly.
   He delights in every detail of their lives.
   Though they stumble, they will never fall,
   for the LORD holds them by the hand.
   (Psalm 37:23-24)

Your Mornings So Far

1. What are some challenges you've faced during the 40-Day Worship Experience?

2. What is happening in your heart, and what is God speaking to you?

3. What changes do you see happening in your life?

LISTEN

LISTEN

Be still and let God speak to you.

Listen to me; listen, and pay close attention (Isaiah 28:23).

"Through this challenge, I have learned that I am a lot more of a busybody than I realized," wrote Nikki, a young woman who took this challenge a few years ago. "I have a busy mind and a busy life. I am always moving, creating, thinking, learning, or talking, but I don't realize it until I sit down and try to quiet my soul. It has become one of the most valuable parts of my day—but not the easiest."

I couldn't agree more. Listening is not easy, especially for some of us. But it is essential in every successful relationship. And when it comes to our walk with God, listening is essential.

A Still, Small Voice

The prophet Elijah was afraid for his life and angry with

God for abandoning him. Elijah had just been used by God to bring a great victory against the false prophets of Jezebel, the evil queen of Israel and the enemy of God. Now, Jezebel had sworn to kill him in revenge. He fled into the desert and prayed to die.

God didn't rebuke Elijah for his self-pity or his emotional distress. He understood Elijah's response and met it with grace: He sent an angel with food and water. Then He told Elijah to go out on a mountainside to meet with God. We read in 1 Kings 19:11-13 (NKJV):

> And behold, the Lord passed by, and a great and strong wind tore into the mountains and broke the rocks in pieces before the Lord, but the Lord was not in the wind; and after the wind an earthquake, but the Lord was not in the earthquake; and after the earthquake a fire, but the Lord was not in the fire; and after the fire a still small voice. So it was, when Elijah heard it, that he wrapped his face in his mantle and went out and stood in the entrance of the cave. Suddenly a voice came to him ...

Often we wish God would speak to us with thunder and lightning, or that a voice from heaven would shout out instructions. If that actually happened, of course, we'd probably pass out.

God does speak to us, but often we aren't listening. Other times we are confused, wondering whether God is actually talking or not. We must learn to hear the "still, small voice" of the Holy Spirit in our heart.

As thoughts enter our mind—the gateway to the heart—we should ask the Holy Spirit who is talking. Our mind processes thousands of thoughts a day, and not all of them are from God.

Earlier, I discussed three destructive sources of thoughts: our flesh, the world, and the devil. Our *flesh*, in the biblical definition of the word, is the old, pre-Christ way of thinking and reacting that tries to sneak back into our life. Fleshly thoughts are described in Galatians as the "passions and desires of [our] sinful nature" (Galatians 5:24). These thoughts are usually characterized by selfishness and a lack of self-control.

> WE MUST LEARN TO HEAR THE STILL, SMALL VOICE OF THE HOLY SPIRIT IN OUR HEART.

Worldly thoughts also compete for our attention. Every culture has certain philosophies, beliefs, and values that contradict God's Word. Not everything our culture teaches is wrong, of course, but when the Bible refers to the "world" in this sense, it is referring especially to these anti-biblical beliefs.

And of course, *the unseen world*—demonic influence originating from the devil—actively targets our mind and emotions. These thoughts are intentionally deceitful, meant to make good look evil and evil, good.

All thoughts are essentially voices. They are not

aimless, passive musings—they take on a life of their own. They speak to us, influence us, and direct us. They sink down into our heart, into the fabric of our being, and subtly influence everything we do.

I know what it's like to be plagued with certain thoughts and emotions. You probably do, too. They seem to be tailored to our situation and personality. It's as if someone knows our weaknesses and is taking every opportunity to jab at them, hoping to bring us down.

Actually, that's exactly what is happening. The flesh, the world system, and the unseen world are three voices that constantly shout at us in an attempt to lead us away from God's presence and ultimately His plan for our life.

Yet through the noise, if we are listening, we can always hear God's still, small voice.

Speak, Your Servant Is Listening

We must learn to review the thoughts that enter our mind and distinguish God's thoughts from competing voices. This requires practice and the help of the Holy Spirit. God wants to teach us how to tune our heart, which is our receiver, to hear what He has to say. Jesus said, "My sheep listen to my voice; I know them, and they follow me" (John 10:27).

"God's voice" is the conversation the Holy Spirit has with our heart: our mind, will, and emotions. The voice of God speaks to our heart about the things that pertain to life and godliness, illuminating His Word within us.

Samuel was just a boy serving in the temple when he got his first lesson in tuning his ear to the voice of God. The Bible says, "Samuel did not yet know the Lord because he had never had a message from the Lord before" (1 Samuel 3:7). One night, when everyone was asleep, he was awakened by a voice calling his name. He assumed it was his mentor, Eli the priest, and ran to see what he needed. This happened three times, and finally Eli realized it was God calling Samuel. He told Samuel to respond to God by saying, "Speak, your servant is listening" (1 Samuel 3:9).

Samuel had to train his spiritual ear to hear God's voice, and so must we. This does not happen automatically. When babies are born, they are able to faintly recognize the sound of their parent's voices, but that is all. Soon, though, they begin to understand tones and inflections. With time, they understand words; and finally, as they grow older, they are able to carry on conversations. In the same way, our spiritual senses must develop in order to consistently hear and understand the voice of the Spirit.

> THROUGH THE NOISE, IF WE ARE LISTENING, WE CAN ALWAYS HEAR GOD'S STILL, SMALL VOICE.

Don't get frustrated if at times you don't hear God's voice or are not sure what He is saying. It will get easier as you develop a deeper relationship with Him. The very fact that you desire to hear His voice—that you are saying, "Speak, Lord, I'm listening"—brings Him joy.

Wanting to hear God is the first step in learning to discern His voice. When Samuel realized who was speaking to him and voluntarily turned his attention to God, he was able to hear the message God had for him.

God wants to speak to us—He is waiting for us to want to listen. He told Jeremiah, "Call to me, and I will answer you, and show you great and mighty things, which you do not know" (Jeremiah 33:3, NKJV). James says, "Draw near to God and he will draw near to you" (James 4:8). God wants us to be passionate about His presence, as David was: "As the deer longs for streams of water, so I long for you, O God" (Psalm 42:1).

Hearing and Knowing

Keep in mind that hearing God speak is not an end in itself, but rather the means to an end. Our goal is to know God, to have a relationship with Him. Listening and hearing is the path to knowing Him better. This aspect of a relationship with God is a hallmark of Christianity.

Paul declares in Philippians 3:10, "I want to know Christ." Knowing God was His highest pursuit. The Greek word "to know," *ginosko*, is more than an intellectual knowledge—it speaks of knowledge by experience or by close relationship. Paul didn't want to just know *about*

God. He wanted *authentic friendship with Him.* This type of knowledge comes from ongoing communication.

Ongoing communication will be both planned and unplanned. Human relationships work this way as well. Sometimes we schedule time to speak with people, and sometimes we have spontaneous, informal conversations. In the same way, if we are truly listening to God, it will carry over from our devotional time to the rest of our day. We might be driving, talking to someone, taking the kids to school, or enjoying a vacation, when suddenly we will find ourselves in inner communication with God.

Listening is more of a heart posture than a one-time act. If we have a listening heart, we will hear Him when He speaks. The more we practice listening to His voice during our devotional time, the easier it will be to hear Him when He wants to get our attention at other times throughout the day, even when we least expect it.

Tune Out to Tune In

We often get so busy and rushed in life or so preoccupied with natural things that we can't clearly hear the voice of the Holy Spirit. One of the most important steps in hearing from the Lord is simply learning to listen. It is slowing down, tuning out distractions, and tuning in to what God is saying.

Remember, the world, the flesh, and the devil will try to "jam the frequencies" by keeping us busy, compromised in sin, distracted with fears and anxieties, or weighed down with guilt and shame. These things interfere with our ability to hear God clearly. The enemy of our soul doesn't want us to experience the joy of walking in a deep, intimate fellowship with God.

Even good things such as family, education, work, and goals can begin to crowd out a relationship with God if we aren't careful. God warned the church at Ephesus that their love had grown cold (Revelation 2). Over time, they had left behind their passion for God. They weren't evil and they weren't living in sin—they had simply begun to grow distant from God.

> CALL A TIME OUT AND FIND A QUIET PLACE TO GET ALONE WITH GOD.

The first thing I recommend we do is stop. Stop everything. Get off the treadmill of life. Call a time out and find a quiet place to get alone with God.

The 40-Day Worship Experience affords us this time in the morning to "tune out" and "tune in." Tune out busyness and tune in peace. Tune out temptation and tune in grace. Tune out condemnation and tune in forgiveness. Tune out fear and tune in faith.

Samuel listened in the quiet hours, when most people were asleep. Jesus got up early, before daybreak, and met with the Father (Mark 1:35). The place where Jesus went was called a solitary place—a place that was quiet and undisturbed. Even Peter did not know where Jesus was and had to look for Him (Mark 1:36). Before the hustle and bustle of life and all the daily demands start, we must spend time alone with the Lord.

All These Things

Matthew 6:33 says, "Seek first the kingdom of God and His righteousness, and all these things shall be added to you" (NKJV). Get ready, because as you listen to God through His Word and by His Spirit each day, He will add blessing upon blessing to your life (Psalm 1:2-3).

What are these blessings? One of the greatest blessings God adds is *peace.* As we listen to God daily, our inner world will start to calm down. Our circumstances might not change at first, but we will find peace and joy just sitting at His feet, listening, like Mary did. God's peace will mount a guard around our heart and mind (Philippians 4:7). This supernatural peace is God's presence filling our heart. Peace is a part of the Kingdom of God, and we cannot thrive without it. In the absence of peace, anxiety and fear gain entrance to our heart.

Another blessing that comes when we listen to God is a *deeper awareness of His love for us.* His unconditional love is the only love that can fill the void in our hearts. We are the object of His love, and that realization gives us the strength to face any challenge or obstacle throughout the day. Our self-esteem and self-identity are not defined by worldly values or relationships, but by the fact that God loves us.

A third blessing that comes from listening to God is *supernatural understanding of the Bible*. The Word of God will come alive and speak to our hearts in a fresh way. We will find Scriptures coming to mind throughout the day, just when we need them. This can be for correction, direction, wisdom, counsel—whatever is needed.

Fourth, listening to God daily brings *character transformation*. The Holy Spirit's creative power works in us to produce God's will. The voice of the Spirit produces the fruit of the Spirit (Galatians 5:22-23).

> HE CAN ACCOMPLISH MORE IN A MOMENT OF DIVINE INTERVENTION THAN WE CAN IN A LIFETIME OF STRIVING AND STRUGGLING ON OUR OWN.

A fifth blessing we receive through listening is a *renewed mind*. Clutter that has been in our hearts is cleared out. The static goes away and God's thoughts flow through our minds. We can enjoy the mind of Christ.

Sixth, listening to God *releases the gifts of the Spirit* (1 Corinthians 12:7-11). When we are attentive to His voice, God works in us and through us in supernatural ways. He can accomplish more in a moment of divine intervention than we can in a lifetime of striving and struggling on our own. Walking with God is an exciting adventure, and listening to Him is a key to walking with Him.

Finally, listening to God allows us to receive *direction from Him* in our day-to-day life. Our decisions, values, words, and actions will always be better when we allow Him to guide us.

One final recommendation: as you listen to God during the 40-Day Worship Experience, be prepared to write down what He speaks to your heart. This could include verses, applications, thoughts, impressions, pictures, phrases, and so on. You will want to remember what God says to you in order to put it into practice the rest of the day.

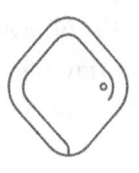

LISTEN

Chapter Summary

This chapter describes the importance of listening to what God is saying. Listening takes concerted effort on our part. I have heard that we think between 20,000 and 60,000 thoughts a day. That is a lot of data considering there are only 86,400 seconds in a day. In the midst of this barrage of information and analysis, we must learn to hear God's voice.

It is vital that we discern God's voice over other voices that enter our minds. Jesus said, "My sheep know my voice"(John 10:27). The 40-Day Worship Experience is an opportunity to cultivate a listening ear that recognizes God's voice.

This starts in the morning as we surrender our will and life to our Creator, the lover of our soul. When we respond to His love and mercy, our hearts are tuned to a divine frequency. We become more receptive to the Holy Spirit who brings to mind the Word of God and puts thoughts in our mind regarding the day: a person to call, something to remember, a warning, a conviction, and so on.

Remember, your mind is the source of your decisions and actions. That is why what you think is so important. Learn to listen to God's "still small voice" and ignore all the other voices. These God-thoughts will lead you into righteousness, peace, and joy.

Questions for Discussion

Take a few moments to pray this prayer, then answer the following questions.

"Jesus, I desire to hear Your still, small voice. Help me quiet my heart so I can hear You clearly. Let me be attentive to Your Word and aware of what the Holy Spirit is saying. Throughout the day, remind me to pause and refocus on You. Make my heart sensitive to Your voice, able to discern and reject any negative voices that I hear. Let me be more and more aware of Your Presence. Hearing You is the desire of my heart!"

1. Have you noticed a difference in your ability to hear God's voice since beginning the 40-Day Worship Experience? In what ways?

2. Is anything interfering with your ability to hear God's voice? How could you become more aware of what He is saying?

2. Identify the three enemies that compete for your thoughts. How is your thought life being affected?

4. Read 2 Corinthians 10:3-5. What does this passage mean to you?

   We are human, but we don't wage war as humans do. We use God's mighty weapons, not worldly weapons, to knock down the strongholds of human reasoning and to destroy false arguments. We destroy every proud obstacle that keeps people from knowing God. We capture their rebellious thoughts and teach them to obey Christ. (2 Corinthians 10:3-5)

Your Mornings So Far

1. What are some challenges you've faced during the 40-Day Worship Experience?

2. What is happening in your heart, and what is God speaking to you?

3. What changes do you see happening in your life?

OBEY

OBEY

Respond in faith to God's specific direction.

Teach me your decrees, O Lord; I will keep them to the end. Give me understanding and I will obey your instructions; I will put them into practice with all my heart (Psalm 119:33-34).

Once you discern God's voice, the next step is to obey. God spoke to Abraham and told him to set out on a journey with an unknown destination. Abraham responded in faith and did what he was instructed. As a result, the Bible calls him the father of all who believe (Romans 4:16). On another occasion, God told him to sacrifice the life of his beloved son, Isaac (Genesis 22). Abraham again demonstrated his faith by being willing to obey, although God was only testing him and stopped him from carrying out the sacrifice. Abraham's faith is seen in his obedience to God's voice.

Intimacy and Faith

Faith is our response to God's word to us. Like Abraham, we demonstrate our faith every time we obey God.

Faith is far more than willpower, however. Faith is a direct result of intimacy with God. The closer we walk with Him, the greater our faith will grow. Knowing God better leads to trusting Him. If we find ourselves lacking faith, the answer is not to try harder—it is to draw closer to God and to know Him better.

As we give our heart over to His leading, we hear His voice more and more clearly. Learn to listen for the prompting of God and respond with faith. This is the greatest adventure imaginable—a life led by God.

Walking in the Spirit

As we come to know God better, our desire to please Him grows. We long for a lifestyle characterized by purity and holiness. But the reality is that we still have sinful tendencies, and we often find ourselves doing the opposite of what we want.

As we just discussed with the issue of faith, the answer to living in purity and holiness is not trying harder. That only produces self-righteousness and pride at first, and ultimately condemnation and guilt when we realize we can't measure up.

The best way to pursue holiness is to focus on

following God, not on defeating sin. Through Jesus, God already provided us with freedom from both the penalty and the power of sin. Sin is simply not as big a problem as we tend to think. Purity and righteousness will be a natural result of following God. We don't have to force anything—we simply respond to God's leading each moment of the day.

The Bible sometimes uses the phrase "walking in the Spirit" to refer to a lifestyle of obedience. The beautiful thing about this phrase is how it communicates the need for relationship. Obedience is not "walking in law" or "walking in willpower" or "walking in good deeds." It is walking in the Spirit. It is an ongoing, personal, intimate, and growing relationship with God through the Spirit.

One of my students, a husband and father named Mark, wrote this:

> *Initially I had a tough time getting up. My alarm would go off, and I would hit the snooze button until my wife got tired of it and forced me to get up. After a while though, I really started to look forward to my time alone in the morning with God. The time I spend in the morning has helped me get closer to my wife and children as well. I find that I am more patient with my children and I cherish my wife more. I look forward to sharing the insights that I got during my quiet time with her, and this sharing has helped us become closer.*

God will direct us as we daily surrender our lives to Him and develop an intimate knowledge of His will. This is the reality of walking in the Spirit that Galatians 5:25 describes. The word "walk" in this verse is used in the military sense of staying in cadence—specifically, to keep in step. This is accomplished through an intimate relationship with the Spirit of God. Life is lived out in a sequence of moments. In each and every one of those moments, we are to be in constant fellowship with the Creator. He wants to guide our every movement to accomplish the tasks at hand.

An ongoing sensitivity to God's leading is required to enter this moment-by-moment walk. The more time we spend with Him on a day-to-day basis, the more clearly we will begin to hear the still, small voice of the Spirit and know the timing of His will.

Hearing and Seeing

We must have the ears and eyes of our heart open to God, expecting to hear and see Him and being ready to obey.

We can prepare our heart to receive from the Lord by knowing His Word, by taking time to listen to the Holy Spirit, and by desiring to hear from Him. Psalm 37:4 says, "Take delight in the Lord, and he will give you your heart's desires." As we spend time with God, He places His desires in us. His heart becomes our heart. This is the foundation of hearing His voice and becoming a good listener.

Hearing from God requires a dose of humility. He doesn't always tell us what we expect to hear. Surprisingly, the Pharisees could not see Jesus for who He was, despite the fact that they were the spiritual leaders of Israel and had exhaustive knowledge of the law. They were blinded by their own pride. This caused them to think they were doing right, when in fact they were in direct opposition to the plan of God.

If we are alert to the promptings of the Spirit, we will discover amazing opportunities in life that we would have otherwise missed. In Acts 8:26-40, Philip was directed by an angel to approach an Ethiopian eunuch who was riding in a chariot. Philip was able to hear and see, and then he chose to obey. He ran up to the man and asked if he knew what he was reading. The eunuch responded that he was reading out of the book of Isaiah, but he did not understand it and needed an explanation. Out of nowhere, a perfect opportunity to share the gospel had appeared. Philip explained to the Ethiopian eunuch what he was reading, and the eunuch was gloriously saved and baptized. This is a clear example of hearing the prompting of God and obeying.

> IF WE ARE ALERT TO THE PROMPTINGS OF THE SPIRIT, WE WILL DISCOVER AMAZING OPPORTUNITIES IN LIFE THAT WE WOULD HAVE OTHERWISE MISSED.

Timing

In the listening and obedience process, it's important to understand the time element. God sees far into our future. Some of the things He shares with us are for right now, while others are for a later date.

Mary, the mother of Jesus, understood this dynamic. When the angel Gabriel told her she would have a baby and who He would be, she was understandably amazed. But she responded with humility and faith, recognizing that the complete fulfillment of the promise would not happen immediately. "I am the Lord's servant. May everything you have said about me come true" (Luke 1:38).

Luke 2:19 says that after the visits by the shepherds and wise men, "Mary kept all these things in her heart and thought about them often." A few verses later, after a twelve-year-old Jesus was found teaching in the temple, we read, "And his mother stored all these things in her heart" (verse 51). Again, Mary realized that God was revealing things to her that were important but that didn't require immediate action.

This is why it is important to write down what God speaks. Some of the things He tells us are to be done right now, and other things will be hidden in our heart, to be accomplished later. The Holy Spirit will help us know the difference.

God enjoys sharing His plans with us. As parents, we tell our kids about our vacation plans because we love watching their joy and anticipation. I believe God also likes it when we get excited about the future He has promised us. He did this for Abraham when He took him outside and showed him the stars (Genesis 15).

God often shares things with us that He intends to do, rather than things that He expects us to do. That's an important distinction. Like Mary, we need to have an attitude of faith and humility when God speaks to us. At the right time, God will open the doors. If we are prompted to do something, then of course we obey. But sometimes the best way to obey is simply to wait and trust.

Courage

The first miracle in the New Testament occurred at a wedding Jesus was attending (John 2). The host of the wedding had run out of wine, a great embarrassment in that culture. The servants went to Jesus' mother and asked what should be done about it. She said to do whatever Jesus told them to do. Jesus directed them to fill jars with water and bring them to Him. It was an odd request, but they obeyed—and Jesus soon turned the water into wine.

I have heard it said that often God asks us to do the ridiculous before He does the miraculous. That doesn't mean we should do bizarre things all the time, hoping for a miracle—it just means be obedient, no matter what He asks us to do.

This requires faith and courage. The Apostle Paul asked the churches to pray that he would have boldness to share the mysteries of Christ to others (Ephesians 6:19). When we hear His voice and discern that it is time to act, we must obey with boldness. Then the ordinary can become the extraordinary through the miracle-working power of God.

David experienced this in the fight against Goliath (1 Samuel 17). David responded to God's leading with faith and courage, and God did the rest. Peter also experienced miraculous results at the Sea of Galilee when he got out of the boat at Jesus' command and walked on water (Matthew 14:22–32).

> ON THE OTHER SIDE OF OUR OBEDIENCE LIES BLESSING.

It's interesting that in the story of Peter walking on water, it was Peter who took the initiative to ask for the miracle; however, he didn't do something that would be foolish in the natural without a clear word from God. We run into problems when we go to one of two extremes: refusing to ever step outside of our comfort zone even when God speaks, or making rash choices in the name of faith but without a word from God.

The devil does not want us to obey God because he knows—often better than we do—that on the other side of our obedience lies blessing. His primary tactic to hinder our obedience is not temptation to sin: it is temptation to mediocrity. He uses regrets of the past and fears of the future to paralyze us in the present. We settle for playing it safe, for maintaining, for barely getting by.

That was the attitude Saul and his entire army had when threatened by Goliath. They were paralyzed by fear.

Satan is a bully who has no power except intimidation, deception, and lies. Unfortunately, we often pay more attention to his loud, empty threats than to the still, small voice of the Spirit. Do not listen to the devil's voice—listen only to God! Then obey with faith and courage. The same God who gave David power to overcome the giant is with you and for you.

God leads, and we follow. God initiates, and we respond. Jesus said, "If you love me, obey my commandments" (John 14:15). He also said we were to deny ourselves, pick up our cross, and follow Him (Matthew 16:24). We don't have life all figured out and we never will. God does, though, and He is faithful to lead us every step of the way. One day we will look back and see His hand at work in each milestone and turning point.

You are entering a new era in your walk with God. Through the 40-Day Worship Experience, you are getting to know God better, hearing His voice more clearly, and learning to follow His leading. The rest of your life is an adventure with Him.

OBEY

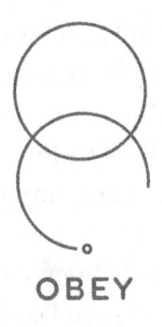

Chapter Summary

Jesus said, "Loving me empowers you to obey my commands" (John 14:15 TPT). James tells us to not just listen to God's Word, but to do what it says (James 1:22).

There are three keys to obedience: hearing God's voice through the Word and the Holy Spirit; discerning God's timing for each situation; and having boldness to step out in faith and do what is being asked of you.

True faith produces obedience. If we are able to hear, then we must be willing to obey. This is how we walk in the Spirit as described in Galatians 5:25: "Since we are living by the Spirit, let us follow the Spirit's leading in every part of our lives." Our obedience demonstrates we are in a dynamic, ongoing relationship with the Creator of the universe.

We are called as believers to walk with God. This is what makes the Christian life so exciting. Nothing brings more fulfillment than enjoying intimacy and closeness with God and doing His will.

Questions for Discussion

Take a few moments to pray this prayer, then answer the following questions.

"Jesus, I am excited to do Your will. Today, I pray for boldness and strength to do what You say. Teach me to respond to You in faith and walk with You every day. I trust You to guide me down Your path for my life. Correct me if I get off track and try to lead myself. Keep me from leaning on my own understanding. Your ways are higher than my ways, and I want to follow Your ways today. My heart desires to lovingly respond to You and obey Your gentle voice. Thank you for leading me."

1. How does our intimacy with God relate to our obedience? See John 14:15.

    Loving me empowers you to obey my commands. (John 14:15 TPT)

2. We discussed how obedience has three ingredients: hearing God's voice, discerning the correct timing, and boldness to obey. Share your thoughts on these three areas and some examples from your own life.

3. Read Galatians 5:25 aloud. What does this verse mean to you?

   Since we are living by the Spirit, let us follow the Spirit's leading in every part of our lives. (Galatians 5:25)

4. Read Acts 8:26–39. How does Philip exemplify listening to God and allowing Him to guide our steps?

Your Mornings So Far

1. What are some challenges you've faced during the 40-Day Worship Experience?

2. What is happening in your heart, and what is God speaking to you?

3. What changes do you see happening in your life?

REVIEW

Surrender
Place yourself in God's hands and surrender your will to His will.

Celebrate
Listen to worship music and enjoy who God is and what He has done.

Meditate
Reflect on the Scriptures and let the Holy Spirit apply them to your life.

Open
Allow the Holy Spirit to bring healing and change to specific areas of your life.

Dedicate
Commit your day to God's use and ask for His help.

Listen
Be still and let God speak to you.

Obey
Respond in faith to God's specific direction.

SURRENDER PRAYER

40-DAY WORSHIP EXPERIENCE JOURNAL

SURRENDER PRAYER

There is something about surrendering ourselves to God that opens up our hearts and souls to receive whatever we need from Him.

The Surrender Prayer is an optional tool to help focus your mind and heart during your time with the Lord. This prayer was birthed out of my journey of meeting with the Lord in the mornings. Even today, I read through this prayer daily. Over the years, I've added to it and changed it as the Holy Spirit has led me. People have shared with me that the Surrender Prayer has become a much-loved part of their daily routine as well.

There are two versions of the prayer: the original, full version and a shorter one. Since the prayer is long, you may choose to use only part of it or to read the short version. Also, feel free to change it or add to it, or even to write your own surrender prayer. The Scripture references that inspired each phrase are included so you can look them up if you'd like to read more. They are just a few of the countless promises and affirmations in God's Word.

SURRENDER PRAYER (SHORT VERSION)

Heavenly Father, good morning!
Ephesians 2:18

Thank You for being with me, around me, and in me by Your Holy Spirit.
Romans 8:16

Jesus, I trust You.
Proverbs 3:5, 6

Jesus, I love You.
Matthew 22:37

Jesus, I need Your help today.
Psalm 46:1

I willingly surrender my heart to You.
Romans 12:1

Thank You for leading and guiding me by the light of Your Word.
Psalm 119:105

SURRENDER PRAYER (FULL VERSION)

I. FATHER

Heavenly Father, good morning! Thank You for this new day. I choose, with excitement and anticipation, to surrender my heart (mind, will, and emotions) to Your unfailing love (Psalm 143:8). I'm offering my body, soul, and spirit as a living sacrifice to You in the name of Jesus (Romans 12:1; Ephesians 2:18). Help me to quiet my heart before You (Psalm 62:1) and receive Your love.

I focus now on all the things that are in heaven (Colossians 3:1). I come boldly into Your Presence, asking You for grace and mercy to help me today (Hebrews 4:16). Your power and love fill me, surround me, and protect me (Psalm 46:1). Thank You for supplying my daily bread (Luke 11:2-3) and for satisfying my deepest need to be loved (Philippians 4:19). Your unfailing love is better than life itself (Psalm 63:3).

Father God, I trust You! You are my fortress and shield (Psalm 46:1) and my hiding place (Colossians 3:3). I am always welcome with You, and I can run to You for safety (Proverbs 18:10). Thank You for holding me in Your arms and being my place of rest and safety (Psalm 68:19). I respond to Your love (Psalm 27:7-8). I humble myself under Your mighty hand (James 5:8). Please teach me Your ways (Isaiah 55:8) and reveal Your heart to me (Jeremiah 33:3).

II. SON

Jesus, thank You for caring so deeply for me that You would sacrifice Yourself on the cross for me. I fix my gaze on You, knowing that You are the author and finisher of my faith (Hebrews 12:2). I open my heart to You (Revelation 3:20).

Thank You that I am seated with You in heaven (Ephesians 2:6). Help me to see the things I face from Your perspective. I cast all my worries, fears, regrets, and anxieties on You (1 Peter 5:7). Please forgive me and cleanse me from all wrong thoughts, feelings, and actions. I choose to also forgive, release, and bless those who have offended or hurt me (Matthew 7:1-3). Please open my heart to Your compassion and concern for those I encounter today.

Help me not to grumble or complain about anything (Philippians 2:14) or compare myself to others (2 Corinthians 12:9). Let Your purposes for me be done today on earth as they are in Heaven (Matthew 6:10). In my weakness, I stir my faith that You can move mountains in my life and in the lives of those around me (Mark 11:23).

Thank You for all You are, all You've done, and all You are going to do. You are the same yesterday, today, and forever (Hebrews 13:8). In You, I live and move and have my purpose for living (Acts 17:28). My life is not my own, for You have purchased me with a great price (1 Corinthians 6:19).

Jesus, I trust You.
Jesus, I love You.
Jesus, I need Your help.

III. HOLY SPIRIT

Thank You, Holy Spirit, for leading and guiding me. Please breathe on me afresh today. Thank You for delivering me from the evil one (Matthew 6:13) and all the temptations that are lurking in me and around me (Colossians 3:5). Help me to focus my thinking on You (Romans 8:12; Philippians 4:8). Keep me from ego, pride, self-promotion, or discouragement today. (Proverb 3:5-6).

Thank You for the promise that I can hear Your voice (John 10:27). Help me to hear, see, and respond to what You are saying and showing me (Mark 4:9; Luke 10:23). Teach me to listen to Your still, small voice amid all the other noises (1 Kings 9:11-13).

Let the Bible come alive to me. Reveal the spiritual and natural gifts I have and continually train me how to use them (Psalm 18:32-35). Thank You for being my mentor, coach, and friend (John 15:26) and for guiding me continually. Place upon me the full armor of God that I might fight the good fight of faith (Ephesians 6:9-12). Keep me in the tension of Your purposes, walking securely on the path that has been chosen for me (Ecclesiastes 6:10). Help me not to look back, but only forward, with no regret (Philippians 3:13).

Let Your peace rule and reign in my heart (Colossians 3:15; Philippians 4:7). Help me to be disciplined and to get all Your work done today. Give me the desire and the power to accomplish each assignment (Philippians 2:13). Thank You for revealing the Father's heart of love to me and for being my constant companion.

40-DAY WORSHIP EXPERIENCE JOURNAL

In the next pages, you'll find forty daily readings from Psalms along with blank lines to jot down your thoughts.

As you begin each day, turn on worship music and take a moment to sit quietly in God's presence. Let your heart be fixed on Him. Surrender your will to His and consciously receive His love. Open your heart to His Word and the flow of His presence.

Then, read through the passage slowly, either silently or out loud. You might even read it several times, letting the Holy Spirit speak as you meditate on the Word. If you'd like, underline or highlight phrases that stand out to you. Use the journal to jot down thoughts that come to mind.

Savor the process just like you would a good meal. Don't be in a hurry. Be still. Listen. Let your heart rest in His. Simply be with Jesus.

Finally, throughout the day, think about the passage, allowing it to be planted deeply into your heart.

2.12

DAY 1

> Psalm 1:1–3

1 Oh, the joys of those who do not
follow the advice of the wicked,
or stand around with sinners,
or join in with mockers.
2 But they delight in the law of the LORD,
meditating on it day and night.
3 They are like trees planted along the riverbank,
bearing fruit each season.
Their leaves never wither,
and they prosper in all they do.

*Which advice?
Advice about relationships? $? etc
Have I limited my joy because I have
followed the advice of the wicked?
Currently I am struggling with my
weight, it is sky rocketing & I am
making terrible choices — I seem power-
less to do otherwise.*

DAY 2

Psalm 3:2–8

2 So many are saying,
"God will never rescue him!"
3 But you, O LORD, are a shield around me;
you are my glory, the one who holds my head high.
4 I cried out to the LORD,
and he answered me from his holy mountain.
5 I lay down and slept,
yet I woke up in safety,
for the LORD was watching over me.
6 I am not afraid of ten thousand enemies
who surround me on every side.
7 Arise, O LORD!
Rescue me, my God!
Slap all my enemies in the face!
Shatter the teeth of the wicked!
8 Victory comes from you, O LORD.
May you bless your people.

DAY 3

Psalm 5:1–3

1 O LORD, hear me as I pray;
pay attention to my groaning.
2 Listen to my cry for help, my King and my God,
for I pray to no one but you.
3 Listen to my voice in the morning, LORD.
Each morning I bring my requests to you and wait expectantly.

DAY 4

Psalm 18:1–6

1 I love you, LORD;
you are my strength.
2 The LORD is my rock, my fortress, and my savior;
my God is my rock, in whom I find protection.
He is my shield, the power that saves me,
and my place of safety.
3 I called on the LORD, who is worthy of praise,
and he saved me from my enemies.
4 The ropes of death entangled me;
floods of destruction swept over me.
5 The grave wrapped its ropes around me;
death laid a trap in my path.
6 But in my distress I cried out to the LORD;
yes, I prayed to my God for help.
He heard me from his sanctuary;
my cry to him reached his ears.

DAY 5
2.16.24

Psalm 18:30–36

30 God's way is perfect.
All the LORD's promises prove true.
He is a shield for all who look to him for protection.
31 For who is God except the LORD?
Who but our God is a solid rock?
32 God arms me with strength,
and he makes my way perfect.
33 He makes me as surefooted as a deer,
enabling me to stand on mountain heights.
34 He trains my hands for battle;
he strengthens my arm to draw a bronze bow.
35 You have given me your shield of victory.
Your right hand supports me;
your help has made me great.
36 You have made a wide path for my feet
to keep them from slipping.

He... arms; makes ways perfect; makes me surefooted, knowing where to step; trains; strengthens, supports, widens the way — opening the path of success

DAY 6

[handwritten notes: instructions → perfect, revive the soul; decrees → trustworthy, make wise the simple; commandments → right, bring joy to the ♡]

Psalm 19:7–11

7 The instructions of the LORD are perfect,
reviving the soul.
The decrees of the LORD are trustworthy,
making wise the simple.
8 The commandments of the LORD are right,
bringing joy to the heart.
The commands of the LORD are clear,
giving insight for living.
9 Reverence for the LORD is pure,
lasting forever.
The laws of the LORD are true;
each one is fair.
10 They are more desirable than gold,
even the finest gold.
They are sweeter than honey,
even honey dripping from the comb.
11 They are a warning to your servant,
a great reward for those who obey them.

Commands are clear giving insight for living

DAY 7

Psalm 23

1 The LORD is my shepherd;
I have all that I need.
2 He lets me rest in green meadows;
he leads me beside peaceful streams.
3 He renews my strength.
He guides me along right paths,
bringing honor to his name.
4 Even when I walk
through the darkest valley,
I will not be afraid,
for you are close beside me.
Your rod and your staff
protect and comfort me.
5 You prepare a feast for me
in the presence of my enemies.
You honor me by anointing my head with oil.
My cup overflows with blessings.
6 Surely your goodness and unfailing love will pursue me
all the days of my life,
and I will live in the house of the LORD forever.

DAY 8

Psalm 24:1-5

1 The earth is the LORD's, and everything in it.
The world and all its people belong to him.
2 For he laid the earth's foundation on the seas
and built it on the ocean depths.
3 Who may climb the mountain of the LORD?
Who may stand in his holy place?
4 Only those whose hands and hearts are pure,
who do not worship idols
and never tell lies.
5 They will receive the LORD's blessing
and have a right relationship with God their savior.

GIVE ME...

★ <u>Pure hands</u>

★ <u>Pure heart</u>

DAY 9

Psalm 25:4–6

4 <u>Show me the right path, O LORD</u>;
point out the road for me to follow.
5 Lead me by your truth and teach me,
for you are the God who saves me.
All day long I put my hope in you.
6 Remember, O LORD, your compassion and unfailing love,
which you have shown from long ages past.

<u>All day long</u>
  DO NOT WORRY
     PRAY & GIVE THANKS & TRUST

<u>Even the silly details matter to God</u>
  * Like who can do the work on our house

        MICHAEL JESTER

DAY 10

Psalm 27:7-8

7 Hear me as I pray, O LORD.
Be merciful and answer me!
8 My heart has heard you say, "Come and talk with me."
And my heart responds, "LORD, I am coming."

DAY 11

Psalm 28:6–8

6 Praise the LORD!
For he has heard my cry for mercy.
7 The LORD is my strength and shield.
I trust him with all my heart.
He helps me, and my heart is filled with joy.
I burst out in songs of thanksgiving.
8 The LORD gives his people strength.
He is a safe fortress for his anointed king.

DAY 12

Psalm 30:1–5

1 I will exalt you, LORD, for you rescued me.
You refused to let my enemies triumph over me.
2 O LORD my God, I cried to you for help,
and you restored my health.
3 You brought me up from the grave, O LORD.
You kept me from falling into the pit of death.
4 Sing to the LORD, all you godly ones!
Praise his holy name.
5 For his anger lasts only a moment,
but his favor lasts a lifetime!
Weeping may last through the night,
but joy comes with the morning.

2.24

DAY 13

Psalm 32:7-11

7 For you are my hiding place;
you protect me from trouble.
You surround me with songs of victory.
8 The LORD says, "I will guide you along the best
 pathway for your life.
I will advise you and watch over you.
9 Do not be like a senseless horse or mule
that needs a bit and bridle to keep it under control."
10 Many sorrows come to the wicked,
but unfailing love surrounds those who trust the LORD.
11 So rejoice in the LORD and be glad, all you who
 obey him!
Shout for joy, all you whose hearts are pure!

DAY 14

Psalm 33:15–22

15 He made their hearts,
so he understands everything they do.
16 The best-equipped army cannot save a king,
nor is great strength enough to save a warrior.
17 Don't count on your warhorse to give you victory—
for all its strength, it cannot save you.
18 But the LORD watches over those who fear him,
those who rely on his unfailing love.
19 He rescues them from death
and keeps them alive in times of famine.
20 We put our hope in the LORD.
He is our help and our shield.
21 In him our hearts rejoice,
for we trust in his holy name.
22 Let your unfailing love surround us, LORD,
for our hope is in you alone.

DAY 15

Psalm 34:8–10, 19

8 Taste and see that the LORD is good.
Oh, the joys of those who take refuge in him!
9 Fear the LORD, you his godly people,
for those who fear him will have all they need.
10 Even strong young lions sometimes go hungry,
but those who trust in the LORD will lack no good thing.

19 The righteous person faces many troubles,
but the LORD comes to the rescue each time.

2.27.24

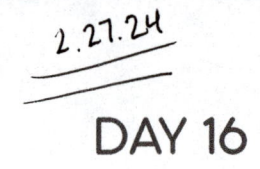

DAY 16

Psalm 36:6–9

6 Your righteousness is like the mighty mountains,
your justice like the ocean depths.
==You care for people and animals alike, O LORD.==
7 How precious is your unfailing love, O God!
★ All humanity finds shelter
in the shadow of your wings.
8 You feed them from the abundance of your own house,
letting them drink from your river of delights.
9 For you are the fountain of life,
the light by which we see.

DAY 17 <u>2-28-24</u>

Psalm 37:23–26

23 The LORD <u>directs the steps</u> of the godly.
He delights in every detail of their lives.
→ 24 Though the<u>y stumble</u>, they will never fall,
for the LORD holds them by the hand.
25 Once I was young, and now I am old.
Yet I have never seen the godly abandoned
or their children begging for bread.
26 The godly always give generous loans to others,
and their children are a blessing.

DAY 18

Psalm 41:1–3

1 Oh, the joys of those who are kind to the poor!
The LORD rescues them when they are in trouble.
2 The LORD protects them
and keeps them alive.
He gives them prosperity in the land
and rescues them from their enemies.
3 The LORD nurses them when they are sick
and restores them to health.

The Lord does everything the only choice the person made was to be kind to the poor.

DAY 19

Psalm 57:1–3

1 Have mercy on me, O God, have mercy!
I look to you for protection.
I will hide beneath the shadow of your wings
until the danger passes by.
2 I cry out to God Most High,
to God who will fulfill his purpose for me.
3 He will send help from heaven to rescue me,
disgracing those who hound me.
My God will send forth his unfailing love and
 faithfulness.

DAY 20

Psalm 57:7-11

7 My heart is confident in you, O God;
my heart is confident.
No wonder I can sing your praises!
8 Wake up, my heart!
Wake up, O lyre and harp!
I will wake the dawn with my song.
9 I will thank you, Lord, among all the people.
I will sing your praises among the nations.
10 For your unfailing love is as high as the heavens.
Your faithfulness reaches to the clouds.
11 Be exalted, O God, above the highest heavens.
May your glory shine over all the earth.

3-3

DAY 21

Psalm 59:16–17

16 But as for me, I will sing about your power.
☆ Each morning I will sing with joy about your unfailing
love. ↳ refresh at the start of each new day
For you have been my refuge,
a place of safety when I am in distress.
17 O my Strength, to you I sing praises,
for you, O God, are my refuge,
the God who shows me unfailing love.

3-4

DAY 22

Psalm 61:1-4

1 O God, listen to my cry!
Hear my prayer!
2 From the ends of the earth,
I cry to you for help
when my heart is overwhelmed.
Lead me to the towering rock of safety,
3 for you are my safe refuge,
a fortress where my enemies cannot reach me.
4 Let me live forever in your sanctuary,
safe beneath the shelter of your wings!

DAY 23 ³⁻⁵

Psalm 62:1–2; 5–8

1 I wait quietly before God,
for my victory comes from him.
2 He alone is my rock and my salvation,
my fortress where <u>I will never be shaken</u>.

5 Let all that I am wait quietly before God,
for my hope is in him.
6 He alone is my rock and my salvation,
my fortress where I will not be shaken.
7 My victory and honor come from God alone.
He is my refuge, a rock where no enemy can reach me.
8 O my people, trust in him at all times.
Pour out your heart to him,
for God is our refuge.

DAY 24
March 6

Psalm 63:1–8

1 O God, you are my God;
I earnestly search for you.
My soul thirsts for you;
my whole body longs for you
in this parched and weary land
where there is no water.
2 I have seen you in your sanctuary
and gazed upon your power and glory.
3 Your unfailing love is better than life itself;
how I praise you!
4 I will praise you as long as I live,
lifting up my hands to you in prayer.
5 You satisfy me more than the richest feast.
I will praise you with songs of joy.
6 I lie awake thinking of you,
meditating on you through the night.
7 Because you are my helper,
I sing for joy in the shadow of your wings.
8 I cling to you;
your strong right hand holds me securely.

DAY 25

Psalm 66:1–4

1 Shout joyful praises to God, all the earth!
2 Sing about the glory of his name!
Tell the world how glorious he is.
3 Say to God, "How awesome are your deeds!
Your enemies cringe before your mighty power.
4 Everything on earth will worship you;
they will sing your praises,
shouting your name in glorious songs."

3/8/24

DAY 26

Psalm 86:1–7

1 Bend down, O LORD, and hear my prayer;
answer me, for I need your help.
2 Protect me, for I am devoted to you.
Save me, for I serve you and trust you.
You are my God.
3 Be merciful to me, O Lord,
for I am calling on you constantly.
4 Give me happiness, O Lord,
for I give myself to you.
5 O Lord, you are so good, so ready to forgive,
so full of unfailing love for all who ask for your help.
6 Listen closely to my prayer, O LORD;
hear my urgent cry.
7 I will call to you whenever I'm in trouble,
and you will answer me.

DAY 27

Psalm 91:1–4

1 Those who live in the shelter of the Most High
will find rest in the shadow of the Almighty.
2 This I declare about the LORD:
He alone is my refuge, my place of safety;
he is my God, and I trust him.
3 For he will rescue you from every trap
and protect you from deadly disease.
4 He will cover you with his feathers.
He will shelter you with his wings.
His faithful promises are your armor and protection.

DAY 28

Psalm 91:5–10

5 Do not be afraid of the terrors of the night,
nor the arrow that flies in the day.
6 Do not dread the disease that stalks in darkness,
nor the disaster that strikes at midday.
7 Though a thousand fall at your side,
though ten thousand are dying around you,
these evils will not touch you.
8 Just open your eyes,
and see how the wicked are punished.
9 If you make the LORD your refuge,
if you make the Most High your shelter,
10 no evil will conquer you;
no plague will come near your home.

3-11-24

DAY 29

Psalm 91:11–16

<u>11 For he will order his angels
to protect you wherever you go.</u>
12 They will hold you up with their hands
so you won't even hurt your foot on a stone.
13 You will trample upon lions and cobras;
you will crush fierce lions and serpents under your feet!
14 The LORD says, "I will rescue those who love me.
I will protect those who trust in my name.
15 When they call on me, I will answer;
I will be with them in trouble.
I will rescue and honor them.
16 I will reward them with a long life
and give them my salvation."

DAY 30

Psalm 92:12–15

12 But the godly will flourish like palm trees
and grow strong like the cedars of Lebanon.
13 For they are transplanted to the LORD's own house.
They flourish in the courts of our God.
14 Even in old age they will still produce fruit;
they will remain vital and green.
15 They will declare, "The LORD is just!
He is my rock!
There is no evil in him!"

DAY 31

Psalm 94:17-19

17 Unless the LORD had helped me,
I would soon have settled in the silence of the grave.
18 I cried out, "I am slipping!"
but your unfailing love, O LORD, supported me.
19 When doubts filled my mind,
your comfort gave me renewed hope and cheer.

DAY 32

Psalm 100

1 Shout with joy to the LORD, all the earth!
2 Worship the LORD with gladness.
Come before him, singing with joy.
3 Acknowledge that the LORD is God!
He made us, and we are his.
We are his people, the sheep of his pasture.
4 Enter his gates with thanksgiving;
go into his courts with praise.
Give thanks to him and praise his name.
5 For the LORD is good.
His unfailing love continues forever,
and his faithfulness continues to each generation.

DAY 33

Psalm 108:1–5

1 My heart is confident in you, O God;
no wonder I can sing your praises with all my heart!
2 Wake up, lyre and harp!
I will wake the dawn with my song.
3 I will thank you, LORD, among all the people.
I will sing your praises among the nations.
4 For your unfailing love is higher than the heavens.
Your faithfulness reaches to the clouds.
5 Be exalted, O God, above the highest heavens.
May your glory shine over all the earth.

DAY 34

Psalm 111:1-5

1 Praise the LORD!
I will thank the LORD with all my heart
as I meet with his godly people.
2 How amazing are the deeds of the LORD!
All who delight in him should ponder them.
3 Everything he does reveals his glory and majesty.
His righteousness never fails.
4 He causes us to remember his wonderful works.
How gracious and merciful is our LORD!
5 He gives food to those who fear him;
he always remembers his covenant.

DAY 35

Psalm 116:1–7

1 I love the LORD because he hears my voice
and my prayer for mercy.
2 Because he bends down to listen,
I will pray as long as I have breath!
3 Death wrapped its ropes around me;
the terrors of the grave overtook me.
I saw only trouble and sorrow.
4 Then I called on the name of the LORD:
"Please, LORD, save me!"
5 How kind the LORD is! How good he is!
So merciful, this God of ours!
6 The LORD protects those of childlike faith;
I was facing death, and he saved me.
7 Let my soul be at rest again,
for the LORD has been good to me.

DAY 36

Psalm 121

1 I look up to the mountains—
does my help come from there?
2 My help comes from the LORD,
who made heaven and earth!
3 He will not let you stumble;
the one who watches over you will not slumber.
4 Indeed, he who watches over Israel
never slumbers or sleeps.
5 The LORD himself watches over you!
The LORD stands beside you as your protective shade.
6 The sun will not harm you by day,
nor the moon at night.
7 The LORD keeps you from all harm
and watches over your life.
8 The LORD keeps watch over you as you come and go,
both now and forever.

DAY 37

Psalm 139:1–6

1 O LORD, you have examined my heart
and know everything about me.
2 You know when I sit down or stand up.
You know my thoughts even when I'm far away.
3 You see me when I travel
and when I rest at home.
You know everything I do.
4 You know what I am going to say
even before I say it, LORD.
5 You go before me and follow me.
You place your hand of blessing on my head.
6 Such knowledge is too wonderful for me,
too great for me to understand!

DAY 38

Psalm 144:1-2

1 Praise the LORD, who is my rock.
He trains my hands for war
and gives my fingers skill for battle.
2 He is my loving ally and my fortress,
my tower of safety, my rescuer.
He is my shield, and I take refuge in him.
He makes the nations submit to me.

DAY 39

Psalm 146:1–6

1 Praise the LORD!
Let all that I am praise the LORD.
2 I will praise the LORD as long as I live.
I will sing praises to my God with my dying breath.
3 Don't put your confidence in powerful people;
there is no help for you there.
4 When they breathe their last, they return to the earth,
and all their plans die with them.
5 But joyful are those who have the God of Israel as their helper,
whose hope is in the LORD their God.
6 He made heaven and earth,
the sea, and everything in them.
He keeps every promise forever.

DAY 40

Psalm 150

1 Praise the LORD!
Praise God in his sanctuary;
praise him in his mighty heaven!
2 Praise him for his mighty works;
praise his unequaled greatness!
3 Praise him with a blast of the ram's horn;
praise him with the lyre and harp!
4 Praise him with the tambourine and dancing;
praise him with strings and flutes!
5 Praise him with a clash of cymbals;
praise him with loud clanging cymbals.
6 Let everything that breathes sing praises to the LORD!
Praise the LORD!

CONGRATULATIONS

You have crossed the finish line! That is an amazing accomplishment.

Now it's time to make a commitment for the future. You have established a great routine in the morning by meeting with God first and learning to take one day at a time. I encourage you to let that be a launching pad for a lifestyle of spending time with God in the mornings. I believe those moments alone with Him will change you forever.

I also invite you to encourage someone else to do the 40-Day Worship Experience with you. Share your testimony with them of what God has done in your heart through the experience, and invite them to try it with you. As you go along, coach them into a deeper, more intimate walk with God by meeting with Him daily.

For more information and encouragement, please visit our website, www.bewithjesus365.org.

Mark Jones

APPRECIATION

First and foremost, thank you to my Lord Jesus Christ, who is at the center of this book.

This book would not have been possible without the support and contributions of many people.

To my wonderful wife and best friend, Susan, and to my family: Thank you! I adore each one of you.

To Pastor Frank Damazio: you are my pastor and I deeply appreciate you. Thank you for your leadership and friendship in my life.

To Dennis Jackson and Wayne Little: thank you for your listening ears and feedback that helped shape these ideas.

To Justin Jaquith: thank you for rewriting my words into a more readable form.

To Larry Asplund: thank you for your help and encouragement.

To our personal intercessors who meet every month and have prayed faithfully to see this project to completion: I am so grateful for your support.

There is not enough room to thank everyone who has spoken into my life over the years, but I am a better person because of your influence. I am blessed to be surrounded by so many friends.

ABOUT THE AUTHOR

Dr. Mark Jones is the prayer pastor and an elder at Mannahouse in Portland, Oregon. Mannahouse is a thriving, multi-site church with worldwide influence that Mark has been a part of for over forty years. Besides overseeing the prayer ministries, he has taught a prayer and evangelism class at Portland Bible College and assists in the leadership of Breakthrough, a recovery program. Mark loves the local church and is passionate about seeing people develop a vital relationship with their Creator.

Mark did his undergraduate work at Oregon State University, where he received a degree in science. He went on to graduate from Oregon Health Science University with a D.M.D. and worked as a dentist in the Portland area for thirty-six years until his retirement.

Mark enjoys cycling and other health and fitness activities. Like any good Northwest native, he loves a cup of coffee with friends. He lives in Portland with his wife Susan. They have four adult children and six grandchildren (and counting!).

Made in United States
Orlando, FL
07 February 2024